PLAIN OLD AGENT

[signature]

Diana --
Thanks for reading!
We hope you enjoy it.

Scott Fasnacht

PLAIN OLD AGENT

Reflections on the Siege at Waco
and My Career with ATF

•

DAVID DiBETTA
WITH SCOTT FASNACHT

Acclaim Press
MORLEY, MISSOURI

Acclaim Press
— Your Next Great Book —

P.O. Box 238
Morley, MO 63767
(573) 472-9800
www.acclaimpress.com

Book Design: Devon Burroughs
Cover Design: M. Frene Melton

Library of Congress Control Number: 2015910367
ISBN-13: 978-1-942613-12-1
ISBN-10: 1-942613-12-1

First Printing 2015
Printed in the United States of America
10 9 8 7 6 5 4 3 2 1

This publication was produced using available information.
The publisher regrets it cannot assume responsibility for errors or omissions.

Contents

INTRODUCTION

When I first began working for the Bureau of Alcohol, Tobacco, Firearms and Explosives (ATF), I attended a going away party for a retiring agent, which is practically mandatory when a colleague leaves the agency. I remember the retiree saying that new agents often told him they wished that they were the ones retiring. He said thoughtfully, *"what a shame; the twenty-plus years of a career passes fast enough."* He was right, it does.

I served the United States Government for a total of 26 years, including stints in the U.S. Army, U.S. Customs, the Internal Revenue Service and nearly 22 years with ATF. My experiences were frustrating and crazy at times. Through it all, one thing never changed. I was always proud of my service, especially as an ATF agent. I only lost one case, and I honestly believe I never did anything to bring shame to the agency or myself; we put a lot of bad people in jail.

I remember being told by one supervisor that the only reason I was never promoted into management was simply because I never got into trouble. He was probably right, but I'm glad the way my life turned out and I'm happy to be where I am today. My wife still likes me, and my boat works.

It's difficult to capture 22 years on the pages of a book. What follows is a diverse collection of stories that, when pieced together, provide some insight into the life of a street agent. "Plain Old Agent" or POA was a term used internally by some ATF management when requesting personnel for a detail. These details needed no special skill other than being a POA! Sometimes my stories make you laugh, and sometimes you'll likely scratch your head and wonder why.

I am thankful for all the experiences. Whether it was a great day or tough day, every one of them reminded me to appreciate everything in my life. So, why write a memoir? What makes my experiences worth sharing?

While at ATF, I worked on some of the biggest investigations the agency undertook, among them the operations with the Branch Davidians in Waco, Texas. In fact, my initial intention was to devote the entire book solely to my Waco experience. I believe I have perspectives into the operation that have not yet been shared and want to ensure that the officers who sacrificed their lives that day are never forgotten. As I looked back at the full spectrum of my experiences as a special agent, I came to believe that whether good or bad, they collectively provide insight into the complex and sometimes infuriating life of a federal agent.

Pride in my work and the job craft of law enforcement was always paramount. I tried staying up-to-date on the latest trends and technology, which included going through the endless number of e-mails people sent, especially after 9/11, since no one wanted to be the person who sat on intelligence information that could possibly have prevented a terrorist act. I practiced hard to always be a good shot and to understand the latest, never-ending changes in the requirements for successfully completing agency paperwork.

Whether on surveillance operations or completing arrests, I cooperated with other agents because I knew what it was like in busy offices, and how hard it was to get law enforcement deals done. I tried never to blame anyone for a mistake, and instead just tried to fix the problem independently. Unfortunately, that probably hurt me more than it helped me, especially during my time at headquarters, where the more problems you bring to your boss, the more problems they think you're solving.

At nearly every step of my career, I spent millions of dollars on behalf of the ATF and stayed well within budgetary requirements, then watched as others, who overspent by hundreds of thousands of dollars, got promoted because their bosses wanted to see them out of that position.

One of my greatest honors was coordinating the 15th anniversary commemoration at the law enforcement memorial in Waco, even though at times I thought only my wife and I would be attending.

From New York to Houston and D.C. to Delaware, I met the most dedicated and hard-working people in law enforcement representing every agency operating in the country. In my stories, my intention is never to offend anyone in any agency, but to provide insight into the many realities—good and bad—we faced together and introduce readers to the characters who influenced our lives day in and day out. I'm sure nearly any officer out there could fill a volume with his or her own crazy tales.

In an effort to protect the actual identities of any colleagues whose names have not been previously published as part of the historical record, I've created fictitious names and applied them throughout this narrative. I believe that's the fair and proper thing to do.

Throughout my years at ATF, I treated everyone fairly, and there were even many times when a defendant thanked me. That's not to say I was a pushover or was too nice. I got what I needed from defendants for each investigation. I always told my trainees; they could go from being nice to mean, but never the other way around. I was usually successful in getting statements from anyone I talked with.

The bottom line is that my career in law enforcement was incredibly rewarding. Sure, there were frustrations that confused and upset me, but over the course of my career, there were many accomplishments as well as opportunities to be a part of history. It was cool. I hope that is the biggest take away from this book.

The work in law enforcement is difficult. I understand many people believe everything they see on television is real. In more than 20 years, I never lifted a single fingerprint off any of the hundreds of weapons, ammunition and magazines I took into custody.

Compiling these stories brought back many memories and the emotions tied to them. Many thanks go to my ATF colleagues with whom I served and with whom I reconnected throughout this project. They played an important role in helping me clarify key moments and verified that my recollections were on track. To my friends Dave, Jerry and Diane, whose critical and valued opinions helped shape the book, I appreciate your candor and insight. This project would not have been possible without Scott Fasnacht who willingly agreed to help me tackle this book. We worked together for countless hours, writing and rewriting, talking and laughing. I'm glad I was able to work with him.

As she has been for more than 23 years, my wife, Judy, has been unfailingly by my side. Her love and support has been unwavering. She's also an amazing proofreader, whose contributions to this book are found on every page. Thank you for your patience and for sharing your tremendous talent on this project.

PLAIN OLD AGENT

Reflections on the Siege at Waco
and My Career with ATF

Chapter 1
NEW YORK CITY

My First Day On the Job

Not that I had been sleeping all that well to begin with, but the blaring alarm startled me and I stumbled out of bed to look outside. It was a little after two in the morning on my first day as an agent with the Bureau of Alcohol, Tobacco, Firearms and Explosives (ATF).

A quick glance out the window confirmed my fears. The weatherman was right for once and my neighborhood was covered with a heavy, falling snow. It was January 4, 1988, and I knew this was going to be a memorable day.

I left my home in Holbrook, NY, around 3 a.m. for the trip into Manhattan – a trip that would typically take about an hour. The trains were running late due to the weather and track condition. I needed to be at the office by 8 a.m. and had been warned against being late.

I arrived in the city around 7 o'clock and began the fruitless search for a taxi. The streets were completely covered in deep snow – an eerie silence muting the city. Seeing not a single vehicle on the streets, least of all a taxi, I retreated back underground and jumped on the subway. I headed downtown to the Division office, which was located in the Post Office building on lower Manhattan's Church Street.

Of course, that early in the morning, the sidewalks had not yet been cleared, so I forged a path over the three blocks between the subway station and the Division office. The snow rose to the middle of my shins. I was wearing my best suit and dress shoes, which offered no traction and added to the already miserable start to my day. By the time I got to the office, my feet were soaked and my pant legs and shoes were covered with snow.

Everybody was late except for me. I sat in the same lobby chair I used on the day of my interview, and was able to see people arriving at their offices. You could tell just by looking at them how miserable it was outside.

When joining any government agency, there is always a ton of paperwork to complete on your first day. I can't begin to tell you what I signed, but I signed everything put in front of me that morning and was then rushed into the office of Bob Creighton, the Special Agent in Charge (SAC).

I had met Creighton during my interview back in July 1987. That was a surreal day. I was called into a conference room at the Division office and was told to sit at the end of a large conference table. I bet 20 people could be seated around it.

At the opposite end, across from me, was the SAC, and to his left and right were four supervisors on each side. All of these men had a serious demeanor as they introduced themselves.

"Mr. DiBetta, you'll be answering a series of questions from us today," said SAC Creighton. "We'll be making a determination over the next couple of weeks as to whether or not we will have an opportunity for you."

"I understand," I said and waited for the first question.

"Who in the hell do you think you are that you believe you can become an ATF agent?" one of the supervisors yelled at the top of his lungs.

This guy is crazy, I thought. I managed to remain calm and spoke about my previous law enforcement experience, my knowledge of New York City, the Island and its people.

I was hoping they were trying to see how I handled individuals with a certain disposition, or if I would get rattled easily. They continued screaming questions at me. Some were rational, and some not so rational. This was the craziest interview I was ever on.

They covered everything from my background to whether or not I played basketball. I must have impressed them, because they waived the written part of the interview and asked me if I was willing to work in New York City to which I quickly said, "yes."

And so here I was.

"Welcome to the ATF, Dave," said SAC Creighton as he greeted me and two other new agents.

"Where are your parents, Dave? Are they here?" SAC Creighton asked.

"Well, my father passed away some time ago and my mother is at work," I replied, wondering what was coming next.

"Why didn't you bring your mother along to your swearing-in ceremony?" he asked.

"Uh, I wasn't aware that I could or should bring her along," I said somewhat bewildered.

"Well, have you met your supervisor?" he asked, setting me up for one more failure.

"No, sir, I haven't," I said.

"Meet Fred," he said turning toward my new boss. "Why didn't you pick up Dave this morning and drive him into the city for his ceremony?"

Oh crap, I thought. *I've just thrown my new supervisor under the bus twice in the first two minutes that I've known him.*

The ceremony itself was very nice and went off without a hitch. Or so we thought. We all learned a week later that none of the photographs taken of the swearing-in ceremony came out. There was no photographic record of this first step in my ATF career.

My first official duty was to get my coat and head back outside to have photographs taken at a local shop located two blocks from the office. So with my feet already wet, we had to walk back out in the snow, find the shop and get the pictures taken for our IDs. I was glad the shop was easy to find and surprised that it was open.

My photo looked as though I was on some kind of death march. My eyes were dark, my hair was wet; it didn't even look like me. But it was good enough, so we headed back to the office to finish up our paperwork and receive the government-issued equipment they had on hand. Having previously worked for U.S. Customs, I had already carried a firearm, so they were able to issue my first ATF firearm—a .357 caliber, Smith & Wesson Model 66, with the serial number of T00103. Of course, they didn't have ballistic vests or any other equipment. I only received the firearm and six rounds of .357ammunition. They told us the rest of the gear would arrive in a few weeks.

It was close to noon by the time we left the Division office and headed to the Melville office from which I would work during the next two years.

"I'm sorry if I got you into trouble back there," I said to Fred, my supervisor, as we headed across town in his GOV (government-owned vehicle).

Looking to change the subject, I turned my attention to the police radio. It looked like two boxes, one stacked upon the other. The box on top had a volume control and a row of five buttons, while the bottom box had a row of six buttons across its front, also all in a row.

"What do those bottom buttons do," I asked, hoping to talk a little shop and learn something. Well, I learned that ATF operated a convoluted network of radio frequencies and repeaters that were supposed to enable agents from across the country to communicate with one another. The top row of buttons controlled frequency and the bottom row controlled the repeater.

"These damned radios never work," Fred yelled. "The f'ing thing is so complicated, I don't know how to use it."

"Oh, okay," I said, and decided I wouldn't ask him any more questions.

We finally arrived at the office by late afternoon, and Fred introduced me to everyone there. He showed me my desk and told me where he wanted it moved.

The top of my desk had been partially used by another agent who wasn't in the office at the time. I removed all of his stuff from my desk and carefully placed it on his desk. As I started moving my desk into place, I knocked over a clay statue that was on his desk.

"Oh my GOD, what did you do?" echoed across the room from the other agents in unison.

"That is the senior agent's prized possession," said Agent Barry. "It was made for him by his son who has special needs."

Oh crap, can this day get any worse? I thought. *This day cannot be over soon enough.*

It turns out I had set myself up to be the entertainment of the office for the rest of the day. The following day, I spoke with the agent whose statue I broke and apologized profusely. He wasn't the least bit upset.

By 4:00 p.m., my day was finally over and I accepted a ride home from Tommy, my training officer. I didn't say one word the entire trip.

I've heard it said that your first day on the job is a window into the rest of your career. I have no idea who gets the credit for that saying, but in my experience it is absolutely true.

So, This is the ATF

After that first day, I hoped things would get better, and they did. After a few days of office work and reading manuals, I was assigned to my first field assignment. I was to accompany Tony, a senior special agent, to execute a search warrant in Brooklyn.

Since I had not yet gotten all of my government-issued equipment, I borrowed a ballistic vest. After a quick briefing on the assignment, I headed out with Tony.

"You must be the new guy," he asked as we walked toward his car. "Stick with me and I'll show you what to do."

It was reassuring to me, because Tony had about 20 years on the job and I was excited for the opportunity to watch how a real veteran officer conducted himself while executing a warrant.

As we walked to the car, I noticed Tony had a pair of white leather gloves, gauntlets such as the ones the cavalry officers would wear in the movies.

"What's with the gloves?" I asked him.

"I'm a Civil War re-enactor and these are part of my uniform," he replied without further explanation.

Having already learned not to ask too many questions, I assumed that Tony had a really brilliant idea. During this time, gloves of any sort were not used very often in law enforcement when going though household items on a search warrant.

We arrived in Brooklyn and were to serve an arrest and search warrant on a local drug dealer who also sold guns illegally. He lived in an apartment on the second floor of a row home located in the middle of the block. Our assignment was to clear that small apartment. We fell in behind the first team making the entry and when they turned up the stairs, we hit the apartment.

We broke down the door, and as we made entry Tony started yelling, "ATF, ATF."

I was thinking that a few months ago I didn't even know what ATF was, so I started yelling, "POLICE."

We were yelling, "ATF, POLICE — ATF, POLICE," as we made our way through the apartment. No one was home, but we found cups of hot coffee sitting on the kitchen table. In all likelihood, the news crews that had set up just down the street tipped off the suspect. Since no one was there, we turned it over to the search teams responsible for executing the property search.

Our primary responsibilities met, Tony reached for the folded gloves on his belt and started heading outside.

Once we stepped out of the apartment, Tony turned to me and said, "This is when the fun starts."

Perplexed and under orders to follow Tony wherever he went, I followed him out onto the street as he walked toward the closest intersection.

I paused at the curb as Tony proceeded into the middle of the four-way intersection and began directing traffic—waving cars through while yelling at the drivers and pretending to kick cars that dared come too close to him.

I couldn't believe what I was seeing.

"Do you need any more help?" I screamed to him over the honking horns of the equally confused drivers.

"No," he replied. "You can go back inside the apartment and help them search if you want."

Well, that sounded like a much better idea than sticking around and watching him play in traffic, so I headed back to see if I could help in any way. As I was walking back to the row home, the case agent grabbed me by the arm.

"Have you seen the CI? Have you seen the CI?" he screamed at me.

The CI is the confidential informant, so I thought that something really bad must be going down.

"No, I haven't seen him," and before I could utter another word he dashed off in a frantic search.

I learned the case agent had given his badge to the CI to wear around his neck so he could get through the police line. And now, of course, the CI could not be found, explaining why the agent was so frantic.

What a knucklehead, I thought as I headed back to the car, my first field assignment under my belt. Not really knowing what to expect, I was happy that no one was hurt. I saw some good and bad things that day, but rest assured, any missteps I saw, I promised myself I would avoid making them in the future.

On the ride back to the office, Tony was excited about our work that day. "That was a great warrant," he said enthusiastically, but never explained what made it so great.

That's odd, I thought. *No perp, no arrest, nothing. What made it so great?* I was tempted to ask Tony what he meant, but never did. I was learning.

Flashing Lights, Megaphones and AR-15

Between doing deals we were assigned to read Manual Orders. Manual Orders are a series of books explaining procedures, how to write reports, to report accidents and the formalities we had to use in dealing with federal firearms licensees. None of it was very exciting, but we more than made up for it when we got out into the field.

Being new at ATF, and working in a busy area like New York, we typically did two or three warrants a week. One of my favorite arrest warrants involved a Chinese gang trying to buy AR-15 rifles and convert them to fully automatic machine guns.

An agent in our office had received a tip from a firearms dealer. He claimed a Chinese national was trying to buy 16 rifles and had asked questions about how to convert them to fully automatic. Once the background investigation was completed on the subjects, it was learned the Chinese national was trying to export the firearms, so ATF notified Customs and brought them in on the investigation.

ATF worked with the firearms dealer and introduced an undercover agent to the Chinese gang, which ultimately led to a deal to exchange the money in a public place.

So here I was sitting outside a diner in Queens. I was in the back seat of a Customs supervisor's G-ride (G-ride is what we called our government cars), a brand new, fully loaded Ford Crown Victoria he just borrowed from the New York District's Customs Special Agent in Charge. Also in the car was Fred, my supervisor. He was riding shotgun, and a brand-new, female Customs agent joined me in the back seat.

We were parked caddy-corner from the diner, but we needed to cross a major intersection—four lanes of traffic in both directions—in order to get to the diner when the deal went down. Our job was to support the cover teams and the undercover agents already inside.

We were in position for well over an hour, when Fred turned around to me and handed me a megaphone.

"Here, DiBetta. Take this along inside in case we need it," he said.

So without further instruction, I grabbed it from Fred. I caught the Customs agent's eye as I set the megaphone on the seat between us and she said, "Do you think I should have brought my gun today?"

Before I could respond, the bust signal was given.

"GO! GO! GO!" blared from the radio.

Fred quickly tried to plug in the police light—the flashing red ball that mounts on the dash—so we could cross the intersection.

The Customs supervisor, who was driving, glanced down at the light as Fred turned it on – just as he began driving into the intersection. He was temporarily blinded and began yelling, "I can't see! I can't see!"

So with the Customs agent's question about bringing her gun still bouncing around in my head, and the Customs supervisor's screams ringing in my ears, we barreled across eight lanes of traffic.

Oh my God, I thought, *we are going to get creamed in this intersection.*

Miraculously, we avoided a collision—at least with another car, anyway. Having crossed the intersection unscathed, we jumped the curb and plowed into a large pile of dirt left by a sidewalk construction crew; at least we were stopped! We all poured out of the car.

As we ran into the diner, it was chaos. People were screaming and running all over the place. It was a wild scene. Fred shot me a look and I quickly got on the megaphone.

"Stay in your seats," I bellowed. "This is the police, stay in your seats." And for the most part it worked. The people calmed down and stayed out of the way.

Except for one guy! He was sitting at the counter and was clearly nervous and agitated. He kept popping up and down from his stool. I warned him to stay seated.

I was the closest agent to him, but I had my revolver in one hand and the megaphone in the other. Not knowing what else to do, I put the bell of the megaphone on top of his head and pushed him back down into his seat. He didn't cause any more trouble.

It was a successful bust. We grabbed the two suspects and began escorting them out of the diner. Suddenly from behind the counter, the diner's owner bolted after us with a handful of receipts for the meals eaten by the undercover agents and the cover teams.

"Who's gonna pay these bills?" he hollered again and again. The Customs supervisor we were with grabbed the bills out of the manager's hand as we left the diner. I don't know if he ever got paid. It was like a scene you'd see in the movies.

Oh, the Things You See From the Fire Escape

At ATF, as in most places I suppose, as people got to know you and saw how you handled yourself, you were given more and more assignments during warrants. For some reason, I got a reputation for being a good climber. As a result, I spent a lot of time on fire escapes across the five boroughs!

Now, it is true at the time I was 5' 10"and 180 lbs. and in high school I was a gymnast. Maybe that explains it?

On one of my excursions, I had to climb up a riot cage—the metal fencing or gate that rolls down to protect the storefront—grab the fire escape ladder and sit on the bottom rung. I hung upside down and reached down to grab the equipment I needed from the officers below, and then I climbed up to the fourth floor of an apartment building. We were working with the New York City Police Department (NYPD) on an investigation of individuals dealing drugs with firearms.

My job was to create a diversion by smashing the window in the suspect's apartment. So I climbed up the fire escape to the fourth floor and steadied myself on a shaky landing that was only about four-feet wide.

Looking down, I saw four New York City police officers all with their firearms out and pointed directly at me. I think they did that in case there was trouble, but it was unnerving because if they started shooting there was no place for me to go but down.

I didn't want to risk yelling to them so I tried signaling to them to holster their weapons. As I was keeping a wary eye on the officers, I looked through the window I was supposed to smash.

I was shocked to see an old woman resting in a chair and then I heard the bust signal over the radio. I could see the old lady getting up, steadying herself on her walker and start heading towards the front door

This is not going to end well, I thought as I grabbed my radio.

"There is an old woman heading towards the front door and I cannot see anybody else in the apartment," I yelled into the radio just as I heard the entry team's RAM splinter the door to the apartment.

Knowing that a diversion wasn't necessary, I didn't break her window, but did watch as the front door flew open and armed agents rushed into the apartment. The poor woman was so shocked, she fell straight back onto the floor—walker and all.

As it turned out, we had the correct apartment, but the subject was not at that address and spent very little time there. He was later arrested in the neighborhood by the NYPD and charged with dealing drugs and a firearm's possession charge.

After my time in New York, I felt like I could have become a New York City fire escape inspector. I could tell how well a fire escape was maintained just by grabbing and hanging on to the first rung. Other agents did not have the same level of confidence as I did on fire escapes. While in New York, I saw some agents try to not complete their assignments because of the fire escape's shakiness. All it took were a few well-chosen words and they would always complete the assignment.

A Bodega Bust

My supervisor, Fred, turned out to be a really nice guy and selected me to be his partner whenever he had big deals or arrest warrants in the city. One day I joined him in exercising a search warrant in a bodega in Brooklyn.

Warrants such as this one were typically based on information we received from paid informants. It happens when people in the neighborhood need money, so they usually contact the different law enforcement agencies with information. Often they would be signed up as an informant. This practice led to many search warrants and arrests and is used by all law enforcement agencies throughout the country.

Before any operation such as an arrest or search warrant, a briefing is usually held to go over the operation's details. This is done to ensure everybody is up-to-speed on his or her assignments and discuss any dangers the subject posed to law enforcement. We'd also go over any intel on what we might expect to find once inside the house, such as location of any firearms, drugs, the presence of any dogs, or if a suspect was inclined to fight.

During this briefing, we were instructed on the order in which we should place our vehicles as we proceeded to the location. When the briefing broke up we headed back to our cars to form the "cha cha line," where we all get into our vehicles and lineup before heading out to serve the warrant.

It was 1988 and the Ford Mustang with a 5.0 Liter engine had just come out. Fred had one as his G-ride! We were about three blocks from the bodega, when suddenly Fred stepped on the gas and pushed that 5.0 engine to its limit.

"Screw this," he said without further explanation, as I was being forced into the back of my seat because of the speed we were reaching!

We easily raced ahead of everyone else in the cha cha line. Fred didn't even look at anyone in the vehicles as we blew past. I am sure there was some kind of chatter on the radio, but I was too concerned about where we were going and how fast we were getting there.

Pulling up to the bodega, he jumped the curb and stopped the car abruptly up on the sidewalk. He scrambled out of the Mustang and ran into the store.

I was just stunned for a second and had no idea what he was doing or what I should do.

Oh crap, there goes my supervisor, I thought. *I'd better follow him.*

Pulling out my revolver, I jumped into the crowd at the store. "Get on the ground, get on the ground," while waving my gun around like a maniac.

There were some patrons who must have thought that I wasn't talking to them and refused to get on the ground. I was able to correct their behavior by putting the barrel of my revolver to the back of one of their necks and screwing it in.

Everyone was on the ground. I was relieved to see Fred emerge from the back of the store carrying a sawed off shotgun, just as the rest of the entry team entered the bodega.

It must have been quite a scene for those guys. I had about 15 people on the ground and my supervisor had the illegal weapon.

"I got this," I said to other agents with a smirk on my face as they came into the room.

We arrested the owner of the bodega, and found no other weapons. We learned later that the owner of the store was also involved in food stamp fraud. He would pay 10 cents on the dollar for food stamps and then cash them out for full value.

It was during this warrant that I realized my supervisor was a nut. And I mean that in a good way. Fred was a great guy and one of the best supervisors I ever had at ATF.

After several months, Fred told me he liked to take me on warrants; he appreciated the way I handled my firearm and myself. I laughed and thought, *if he keeps picking me to partner up with him, I just might have to use it.* I was also learning who was a worker and whom I should avoid. All and all, I felt I was working well with everyone.

A Hard Lesson Learned: My Introduction to the FBI

The first time I worked with another federal agency while serving as the lead investigator involved the FBI. The case was about the theft of a container of fully automatic weapons. They were stolen from JFK International Airport while awaiting an overseas flight.

I received a trace of a machine gun that was recovered in Queens. ATF keeps a record of all firearms sold, or shipped from any manufacturer and importer in the United States. When a firearm is recovered, it is put into the system and a report is generated then sent to the local office to ensure we follow up on the information. This is referred to as a trace. This trace included an incident report that stated the police responded to a "shots fired call." Upon arriving at the house, they came under fire from one of the reportedly stolen machine guns. The police officers returned fire, and rather quickly, the knucklehead shooting the machine gun ran out of ammunition and tried to hide under a car in the garage.

After reading the entire report, I requested all the traces from the theft of the firearms recovered to that point. I believe it was about ten in all. Then I got a map and plotted the location of where each of the firearms had been recovered. I started to see a cluster in a particular area in Queens. Since I did not have any access to the FBI's reports, I had to make contact with the FBI agent working on this investigation.

Being new, I went to my supervisor and showed what I had up to now then told him I wanted to contact the FBI.

"They'll take all your information and you'll get nothing in return," Fred said. "Go ahead and give it a try, but trust me, you'll see."

I guess it was naiveté, but I was certain I was on to something big and I knew I could work with anybody. I contacted the case agent at the FBI and requested to meet with him. All I wanted in return were the names and addresses of their suspects.

People who commit crimes don't usually go far to commit them. They are typically active within a couple miles from the area in which they live. I thought if I could develop a pattern of where the suspects lived in relation to where the guns were recovered, I might have something to go on and further develop the case.

At this point, I'd been with ATF for less than a year and on the morning of my meeting I thought, *I'm a federal agent going to work with another federal agency on my first big case. This is awesome.*

The first meeting went well. I told the FBI agent what I had and my theory was to see if we could develop anything further from the recovery of the firearms. As the meeting came to an end, he reached out to shake my hand.

"I'll be back in touch with you, DiBetta," he said. "I think we'll be able to make some headway on this investigation."

I was feeling pretty good about myself and honestly believed I had successfully initiated a cooperative investigation with the FBI on this case. When I got back to the office I went straight to Fred's office and shared my news with him.

"You won't get a thing from them," he said.

This surprised me, and my pride was a bit wounded. I thought I had established a good rapport with the FBI agent. "I think you're wrong, Fred," I said with a bit more confidence than I wanted.

"Okay, fine," he said, "but you'll see."

After a week I hadn't heard a thing from the FBI, so I tried calling the agent and he never returned my calls. Then the second week went by, then a third and a fourth.

Having to admit defeat, I walked into my supervisor's office. "Fred," I said, "You were right about the FBI; I shouldn't waste my time with them anymore."

Fred just smiled and nodded. To his credit, he didn't say a word and never brought it up again. To my knowledge, nothing else was ever done on this investigation, and I never again shared information with the FBI.

Another Thing or Two About the FBI

A few weeks after all this ended, the FBI called our office, and asked if one of the agents could assist them in an arrest and search warrant for an individual with local mob ties and possible machine gun possession. As one of the new agents in the office, I was sent.

I wasn't sure where the briefing site was, so I gave myself plenty of time and arrived early. I found an FBI agent sitting on a guardrail. We both identified ourselves and started talking.

"How long have you been with the FBI?"

"Oh, about 17 years," he answered.

"Wow, you must have been on a lot of warrants over the years and seen all kinds of exciting things," I said enthusiastically, my inexperience showing just a bit.

"Well, not really," he replied without a glimmer of energy or remorse. "I usually sit all day and listen to wiretaps."

"Do you enjoy doing that?"

"It's a job."

This took me by surprise. I thought being an FBI agent was more exciting. Even though I'd been with the ATF for 14 months at this point, I think I still had the habit of asking too many questions.

"Why are you out here sitting on the guardrail?"

"I have a lousy car and the seats are uncomfortable," he said without looking at me.

My car was right there and comfortable so I offered, "Do you want sit in my car and wait?"

"Sure," he replied.

He climbed in the passenger side of the car and we made idle talk for the next 20 minutes until the rest of his team arrived. The FBI agent in charge called us all together. "Our suspect has mob ties and we believe he is in possession of several machine guns. He has a long rap sheet and a history of arrests for violent crimes," he shared during the briefing. "That's why Agent DiBetta from the ATF is joining us today."

I went with the team to a two-story motel. Built in the early '70s, it was made of red brick and each room featured a big picture window with the door right next to it. The subject's rooms were located on two levels. Since I was not part of the FBI, I was the last one in the line, or stack, as we walked up the stairs to his room, which was also used as the motel office.

The plan was to make entry into the motel office. Like every other room at the place, the door to the office had a large picture window on one side of it and a brick wall on the other. As our team approached to breach the door, the FBI agents lined up in front of the picture window. The window's curtains were drawn, and nobody had any idea what was going on behind them.

What are these knuckleheads doing? I thought. *Here we are going after a reported mobster with a violent past, armed with machine guns and they're all lining up in front of this big picture window.*

Being fairly new to the job, I thought this was crazy. I had to say something.

"Don't you think we should line up behind the brick wall instead of the window?" I whispered.

Without saying a word, they all looked at each other and ran to the other side. I had to laugh. If you had seen this I think you would have laughed, too. We made entry to the room, and thank God, nobody was there.

We searched the office, but didn't find anything. The poorly lit utility room proved to be a little more problematic. It appeared that there had been work performed on some of the metal pipes, leaving a three-and-a-half foot hole in the floor where the pipes poked through. The owners probably had a leaking pipe because the room had a heavy, damp smell.

The warrant was happening late at night, and this was one of the last areas left to search. The FBI agents were gathering around the pipe opening and discussing how they were going to search the hole.

I watched them discuss back and forth for several minutes and then I couldn't stand it anymore.

"Who is going to jump in that hole and look around?" I asked them rather impatiently.

They looked at me and quickly returned to their conversation on who would take the leap into the hole.

"I'll do it," I said not trying to hide my exasperation.

I climbed down into the hole and examined the area with my flashlight. Not finding a thing but metal pipes submerged into the dirt, I pulled myself out and walked out of the room. It was maybe 20 minutes later; they finished the search and we went home.

Now don't get me wrong, there are a lot of good and accomplished investigators in the FBI, but during my time in New York I didn't meet one.

Operation Rum Punch

The ATF has a way of naming all of their big operations, such as "Fast and Furious." One of the more memorable operations for me was "Operation Rum Punch."

In 1989 when the Jamaican gangs were really bad in New York City, ATF decided to roundup of as many of them as possible. My job was to arrest T.B. Means, a man who was ultimately tracked down on the streets of upper Manhattan.

Means was a heroin addict and very skinny—almost to the point where you could take your index finger and thumb and wrap it around his upper arm. Once my partner and I arrested Means, I had him lean over the car. He began to resist and started putting his hands into his pocket. Not certain what he was going to do, I leaned on him in an effort to press him against the trunk of the car. Suddenly, with only one of his arms he began to lift me off of the ground!

"He's reaching for something in his pocket, grab him, grab him!" I yelled to my partner, who did not react to Means' action.

I managed to wrestle Means into a position where I could put the handcuffs on him. It turned out that all he was trying to do was to get rid of the drugs he had on him.

Once I put the handcuffs on him, he starting screaming with pain. Being a heroin user, the handcuffs were causing him extreme pain as the veins in his wrist were so badly scarred from repeated injections.

"Why didn't you help me on the arrest?" I asked my partner.

"I don't like going on arrests," was his only reply.

"What do you like to do? Do you like to shoot?"

"No."

"Do you like to go on surveillance?"

"No."

"Do you like doing the paperwork?", sarcasm oozing out of me.

"No."

"What the hell are you doing in this job?"

He didn't respond. I don't know all the details of his career, but this guy, who didn't like to do anything, rose to the position of Associate Director West and was one of the highest-ranking supervisors in operation "Fast and Furious."

See where ambition takes you!

It took us about 30 minutes to get Means to the office to process him for court. But first, there's always the paperwork. As we were completing the paperwork we were told to write "Operation Rum Punch" across the top of each page.

Means saw me doing this and asked, "What's Operation Rum Punch?"

"It's a roundup of Jamaican gang members," I said without much thought.

Suddenly, Means got highly upset and started screaming, "I am no f'ing Jamaican," and started grabbing for the paperwork.

I had to push him back down in his seat and told him it had nothing to do with him, it was just the way the paperwork had to be done, and this seemed to calm him down a little.

When you arrest someone in New York City, especially as a federal agent, you have to go through the Marshals Service. The Marshals will not take possession of a prisoner until after their initial appearance in court. As the arresting agent, I was responsible for Means until that happened.

Being a heroin addict and not in the best of shape, he started getting the shakes.

"Can you get me something to eat?" he asked me.

"I guess so," I replied with a little uncertainty.

At the time I was a GS 5 working in New York City, one of the most expensive places in the country. I was still living at home and with a GS 5 salary of only $21,000 a year before taxes.

I was so poor that when I was at a bar, I would take my beer bottle into the bathroom and fill it with water just so I didn't have to buy another beer. I just couldn't afford it at the time.

So, here I was on my limited budget, going out to buy this knucklehead lunch. I asked another agent to watch him while I bought a ham sandwich with potato chips and soda. I put the meal down in front of him and with his hands now cuffed in front, he opened the box lunch and lifted the bread. From the look he gave me, you would have thought I just flopped dog crap on the table.

"I don't eat this crap," he said. "Couldn't you have gotten me anything better?"

"No, I couldn't," I snapped back at him. "You probably make more money than I do. If you want to complain, take it up with your public defender!"

What a jerk. If he hadn't touched the sandwich I would have eaten it!

Finally, after about six hours, we took Means before the Federal Magistrate.

As I walked into the courtroom, I saw six or seven Customs inspectors I had worked with at JFK International Airport. The magistrate was not in the courtroom, so I called out to two or three of them by name and started waving.

"Agent DiBetta, you can't talk to them, they're all defendants," said a Marshal as he rushed over to me.

I learned later they were part of a smuggling ring that attempted to get people and contraband through Customs without being searched. After Means' initial appearance before the judge, the Marshals took him away. I never heard of or saw him again.

Paperwork and Prison Guards

I got off training status after my first year on the job. As a gift to my training officer, I went into the supply closet and got him a brand-new red pen like the one he used to review my reports. I know I am not the best writer in the world, but it's a whole different story when writing reports in the law enforcement community.

ATF was no exception. In fact, you needed to adjust your report writing based on the individual reviewing your work. Some people like things one way, and other people did not. At the time we had archaic report-writing requirements.

On case reports, one of the biggest problems was the evidence being footnoted. For example, say a crime happened on a particular date. Some supervisors wanted the footnotes for the incident on that date, while others wanted the date the police report was written or when any physical evidence or photographs were taken of the scene. There were also group supervisors who believed that some evidence should be footnoted under different actions such as the day the report was approved, or the day the crime scene was processed, if it was actually different from the date of the crime.

Personally, I could have cared less how the evidence for the investigation was footnoted. All I wanted was to be consistent. It never was.

Our reports would continually get kicked back for footnoting errors previously approved. We called this "marking territory" just like a dog would do! You have to remember, this was before computers. Everything was done in triplicate and forwarded, and whoever needed that copy took it, and forwarded the original. Many times we'd get these case reports back after the case was adjudicated. We'd spend hundreds of hours a year redoing paperwork by replacing the corrections in the triplicate files on cases that were closed. Who knows how many trees were killed.

ATF has since changed its case report system. I think they did that to keep us busy so we would not be arresting people and creating more paperwork! They had a saying at our agency that was as true back then, as it is today. "Little cases, little headaches. Big cases, big headaches. No cases, no headaches!"

As scary as the paperwork can be, I'll never forget the first time I was truly scared on the job. After an arrest one late night in Manhattan, my partner and I were bringing a suspect to the federal prison in lower Manhattan.

Arriving at the prison, we pulled up to this metal garage door that opened to let you into the carport. As we were waiting, the door opened and a man came out of the shadows wearing a Bureau of Prisons uniform, an oddly short vest covering the lower part of his neck to the top of his stomach and a baseball cap.

He was armed with a short-barreled shotgun aimed right at us! Completely surprised, and not seeing where he came from, we quickly showed our IDs.

"I hope you boys don't mind if I look into your car," he said. His voice had a deep southern accent that echoed in the garage entrance.

"No, not at all," was all we could muster, as I waited for my heart rate to go down!

After a thorough inspection of our trunk and the front and back passenger areas of the car, he let us in. Once we were inside, we all shared a good laugh, but each of us agreed—this guy, who came out of nowhere with a shotgun, scared the crap out of us.

I would swear that he was also missing some of his teeth. I'm only kidding to all my brothers at the Department of Corrections!

Putting New York in My Rear-View Mirror

When an agency tells you they operate with a family-first policy and they constantly state it over and over again, you know they are only trying to convince themselves it is actually true.

That was the case at ATF. ATF did have a family-first policy, but whether they actually applied it or not depended on who you were.

When I began my new agent training in Glynco, Georgia, in April 1988, I met a woman, Pam. We became engaged then later married. She was from Houston and worked for the IRS at the time. I was trying to transfer from New York to Texas on what was called a hardship transfer because we were married and not living together.

I submitted the required paper work in June 1989, and received no word for three months. I submitted a second request, but still no word. Five months later a transfer list came out with the names of three female agents on it.

We were all hired at about the same time, but my name was not on the list. One of the agents was transferred because she was engaged to be married. The second agent got transferred because she was going to get engaged. The third had a boyfriend in a different state.

It was very frustrating; especially from a law enforcement agency that was expected to enforce all laws fairly and honestly. I put in a third request citing the three other situations and compared them to my own. I also reiterated that I was willing to do a low- or no-cost move.

That last request must have gotten the agency's attention. Finally, in December 1989, six months after we were married, they approved the transfer. I was on my way to Texas.

Chapter 2

WELCOME TO TEXAS

It's the Wild West

December 1, 1989, I drove in my 1984, four door, Toyota Corolla packed with items too valuable to ship, from New York to Houston with my brother, Ron. During the drive we talked about work and moving away from New York, but we focused mostly on where were going because this was before GPS. When we arrived in my new hometown, we went straight to the airport so he could catch his flight back to New York.

The plan was for me to meet Pam at the airport and follow her back to our apartment. When I met her at the airport, I gave her my best smile and leaned in to give her a kiss hello. As I kissed her, she turned her head so my lips could only touch her cheek.

As I stepped back totally confused she said, "I don't love you anymore."

I was stunned. "I wish you would've told me sooner," I blurted back at her, trying to maintain my cool. Then I shot a confused glance to Ron and thought, *I would never have made this move to Texas!*

I did not realize marriage is a sport in Texas, not a commitment. Not sure what to exactly say or do, I said goodbye to my brother and followed Pam in my car with her words still ringing in my head.

"What the hell did I get myself into?" I muttered to myself over and over again on the drive.

Since I still had a couple of days before my belongings were to be delivered, I decided to rent a storage space so I had a place to put them. I'd live out of my suitcase at Pam's and see if I could get my marriage back on track.

After a couple days of living with her, things were not getting any better, but at least I had begun working.

On my first day in Texas, I was assigned to a gun group. Within ATF, a gun group was the closest thing we had to a general operations group. We were assigned to cover the southwest part of the city of Houston and were to investigate crimes such as felons in possession of a firearm and explosives violations. It was pretty basic stuff.

Even though I was no longer on training status by the time I left New York and had two years experience, they decided to put me back into training status. At the time I was upset, but then I realized it was done for my benefit because Don, my supervisor, was an alcoholic. The thinking was that I would be better served in training status, than to work for this supervisor.

I was assigned to a training officer, Carl, who already had two trainees—one female, Sue, and one male, Ron. I didn't understand at the time why Carl was such a jerk to me, but after a week it became clear.

When I first met Carl, I told him about my marital status. He, too, was married, but was dating Sue, his female trainee. I guess he saw me as a threat to his relationship with her.

Many years earlier I learned to never have an office affair or romance. It never ends well and is always messy. At one point we had a supervisor who was having an affair with one of the administrative staff. He must have ticked off another administrative assistant, because that woman borrowed a camera from one of the Tech guys and took pictures of the supervisor and his lover and mailed them to their respective spouses. It got really ugly.

Anyway, you can see that Texas really was shaping up to be great… but I'm just getting started.

When I first began working in the Houston office, I wondered why everyone was a little cold towards me. Usually when a new agent arrives, the other agents in the office are very inquisitive and eager to learn all about you—after all, we were investigators. That sure wasn't the case for me when I got to Houston.

It took several weeks for me to learn why. My colleagues thought I was a "plant" from internal affairs! I was the first person ever to be transferred out of the New York Field Division. At the time, it was unheard of to be transferred out of New York for any reason. It was simply too hard to get people to come to work in NYC because of the gap in pay. Honestly, living in New York isn't for everyone. It's a different way of life and for those who aren't originally from the area, it's too much of an adjustment for the agents and their families.

Things Can Only Get Better

This was a low point in my life. My marriage was falling apart, people thought I was from internal affairs, my training officer was a real jerk, and Texas was such a different world. I mean, in Houston, when you went to a department store and someone approached you and asked, "Can I help you, sir?" they actually meant it! In New York that meant you were about to be accused of shoplifting. I guess I was just feeling a little homesick.

After a few days, I was getting back into the swing of things when I received a phone call from a woman named Laura, who said her estranged husband, Danal, had a criminal history and was in possession of firearms. I got a statement from her, checked on her husband's background, and confirmed he was a convicted felon.

That prompted me to get a search warrant, and after writing the warrant I asked Carl for the location of the U.S. attorney's office.

"How the hell am I supposed to know?" he said without looking up.

Now, for weeks all I had heard from him was how great an agent he was and how hard he works, and yet he didn't know where the U.S. attorney's office was? What an idiot.

I asked another agent and we headed out together. We got the search warrant and executed it the next day. There wasn't a single gun at Danal's house.

One of the neighbors later shared with me they were aware Laura told Danal she was talking to the police about him owning a firearm. He actually gave the firearm to a neighbor as soon as he heard we were looking at him—explaining why we were unable to locate it at his house.

During a follow-up conversation with Laura, she explained to me that she was separated from Danal because he was violent towards her.

"Only meet him in public places when he wants to visit your son," I told her over the phone. "And do not tell him where you live."

A few days after that conversation, I received a phone call from Houston's homicide squad. They said they found my name on a piece of paper in the apartment of a murder victim and wanted to know my connection to her. It was Laura. The Houston homicide detective also said one of the neighbors surrendered a firearm belonging to the murder suspect.

I got an emergency trace of the firearm and confirmed it belonged to Danal. It was purchased many years before his felony conviction. I then interviewed the neighbor over the phone and he told me the same story as the homicide detective.

After speaking to the homicide detective again, we agreed I could get a warrant quicker than he could. So I went to the U.S. attorney's office to again appear before the judge—this time to get an arrest warrant for Danal. I told Carl the homicide detectives had a line on the suspect and I was going over to the homicide unit to wait for a call that confirmed his location.

Of course, Carl decided to take Sue as well, and told me he'd be waiting for me in the general area. Remember, this is a time before cell phones—all we had were pagers and police radios.

I arrived at the homicide office, and within 10 minutes the detective received a call from an informant identifying Danal's location. I rode along with the two homicide detectives. Once again, I found myself in the back seat of another law enforcement officer's vehicle. It was around 5 p.m., and we needed to make time in the midst of Houston's rush hour.

We were in an unmarked police car with just a little red bulb on the dashboard, cruising along at about 80 miles-an-hour. We headed west on I-10, weaving in and out of traffic and riding on the shoulder. While driving at this high rate of speed, the detective behind the wheel was receiving pages and actually drove with his knee at one point to take out his reading glasses! That's when I decided to put on my ballistics vest, just in case we were in a collision.

As we approached our target location, we passed the suspect, who was behind the wheel of a car coming at us from the opposite direction.

"It's him, it's him," I yelled. I instantly recognized his face, even with his freshly grown beard.

We immediately turned around and began following him. We were calling for backup, and I was trying to reach Carl on our ATF radios, but didn't have any luck.

As we stopped at the next intersection, our car was able to pass Danal's and cut immediately in front of him, bringing both vehicles to a stop. I jumped out of the rear passenger side of the car and found myself only three feet from the front of his vehicle.

He quickly threw his car into reverse and began backing up his vehicle, trying to get some separation so he could get around us. I raised my pistol and pointed it directly at him just as I saw his upper right arm move, like he was shifting into drive.

Getting into a shooting position, I put my finger on the trigger and was ready to put three rounds into Danal's head if that car moved one inch towards me. He must have recognized my determination, because he immediately threw up his hands.

I moved to the driver's side of the car and yanked the door open. Pulling Danal out of the car, I threw him on the ground and twisted my .357 into the back of his head. Just then a car pulled up and stopped. Typically, when you make an arrest out on the street, the passersby like to gawk. But this total stranger, as he was driving by, actually rolled down his passenger-side window and said, "Officer, I have a shotgun in the trunk. Do you need any help?"

Being from New York, I knew very few people who carried firearms with them, much less in the trunk of their car. I was stunned and couldn't think of anything of value to say.

"No thanks, citizen. I got it under control," I said and waived him on.

I put the handcuffs on Danal and took him into custody. I whispered in his ear that I wished he had tried to run me down. We went to a local police substation, because I had to wait for Carl as well as Don, who also decided to join us at the scene.

While I'm standing with Danal and the two homicide detectives, Don came on the radio and sounded like a drunken sailor. He was so drunk he had actually driven 20 miles past the exit. I tried assuring him everything was wrapped up and he should go back home, but he was determined to find us.

We waited for at least another 30 minutes, when Carl and Sue finally showed up. I was still on the radio with Don trying to get him to our location, but I wasn't having any luck.

Having heard all they cared to hear, the two homicide detectives had enough and took the prisoner back to police headquarters. The rest of us joined them, heading back towards town without any idea of Don's location.

Once we returned to the police station, we met the five-year-old son of the suspect, who was also the witness to his mother's murder. The Juvenile Division conducted his interview and we were briefed on his statement.

The boy said that his father came to the house to pick him up for a visit. That's when Danal and Laura got into an argument. The child then described how his father pulled out a knife and stabbed his mother more than 30 times.

The boy went on to say his mother finally went to sleep and then she stopped bleeding. Danal took the boy to a local hotel where they hid out for a couple of days until the body was discovered.

After the Houston police finished processing Danal, I took him to jail for the night. I came back the next day to take him for his initial appearance in court. Once I had him in front of the magistrate, the U.S. attorney and his defense attorney agreed to immediately hold the probable cause hearing.

This was my first time in a Texas courtroom, and I wasn't sure what to expect. Once I was on the stand, I shared what happened with the U.S. attorney and then he turned it over to the defense. I was on the stand for two hours.

That attorney asked me every question under the sun.

"Do you know where the local bus stops are in that area?" he asked me at one point.

"No. I just transferred here from New York about 30 days ago," I replied.

"Well, how were you able to recognize the defendant? Doesn't he now have a beard?"

"He only has facial hair," I responded with a little frustration. "He still looks the same."

In the end, the suspect pleaded guilty to my charges of a felon in possession of a firearm and got sentenced to two years. On the state murder charges he received 44 years.

About a week after the sentencing, I received a call from the victim's parents. They were concerned they could not find Danal in the prison system. They wanted to serve papers on him so they could gain custody of their grandson.

I explained to them how in the federal system you could go to any prison within the network and he might not even be in the state of Texas. I promised to see what I could do and then call them back.

I found Danal in Oklahoma. I shared the information with the family and they were grateful. They also expressed their appreciation for all the work we did on the investigation.

I wish their daughter had followed my advice and never let that guy meet at her apartment. Since she was considered a federal witness, I had to write a memo to the FBI informing them a witness of mine was murdered. That was one of the toughest memos I've ever written. She was also the only witness I ever lost in that way.

Needing to Clear My Head

After the alcoholic supervisor, getting put back on training status, the training officer from hell, a witness getting murdered, under suspicion of being an internal affairs officer, and given extra assignments, I decided to go back to New York for two weeks. I really considered quitting ATF, which was practically unheard of at the time.

People typically came to ATF from other agencies, not the other way around. In retrospect, I'm glad I went home to be around familiar faces and places. It was on this trip that I talked to Judy, the beautiful woman who would one day become my wife. I got to know her a little better and we agreed to begin communicating on a regular basis.

After that two-week break, I was feeling better about everything and went back to Texas to start again.

It's Amazing What You See When You're Looking

Texas was an interesting place at the time. If you were convicted of a felony and given 10 years, you only served 28 days-per-year. That's 10x28; only 280 days served for a 10-year sentence. Less than one year.

Those sentencing laws were part of the reason federal officers and agencies were appreciated and needed much more in Texas than in New York. Local law enforcement in Texas looked to the federal laws to ensure some serious time for some of the worst criminals in Houston.

On one occasion I was told to assist ATF's Detroit office in locating an individual who had an arrest warrant on him. After receiving the collateral—a request for assistance from another office—our office quickly got a lead that this guy was possibly working in a factory on Houston's outskirts.

I joined three other agents from the office, and headed down to the factory. Once there, Agent Brown went to find a factory supervisor to see if this individual was there.

"Don't bother," I said to him. "There he is."

"What are you talking about?"

I pointed to a group of people standing off to the side on the factory floor. Nearly all of them had their back towards us, prompting Brown to reply, "You're full of crap."

"Our guy is standing right there in the blue T-shirt," I insisted.

He wasn't convinced, but joined me in walking towards the suspect. As soon as he turned around I recognized his face from the photo and arrested him.

With the suspect in custody, we showed him the way out of the plant and headed to our car.

"How did you know this was our guy?" Brown asked.

"Seriously? Only a guy from the north would wear corduroy pants in the summer!"

"Damn, Dave!" Agent Brown said, amazed at my deductive reasoning.

During the extradition hearing, I also pointed out while at the factory the suspect was wearing the same shirt as when he was arrested in Detroit. I recognized it to be the same T-shirt as in the photograph sent to me by the Detroit agent. I brought this to the attention of the assistant U.S. attorney who was helping in this extradition hearing. He couldn't believe it.

"If this is true, I'm going to use this when you're on the stand," he said.

We looked at the Detroit picture together and the T-shirt the suspect was wearing matched! Sure enough, once I was on the stand and finished going through all the pedigree information on this guy, the assistant U.S. attorney asked me if there was anything else that could identify this individual.

"Yes," I said. "His T-shirt matched the arrest photo I was given by the agent in Detroit."

"Objection!" yelled the defense attorney, who was then granted a quick sidebar by the judge.

Walking back to his seat, all the defense attorney could do was shake his head. We won that hearing, but I'll never forget how stupid that guy was for still wearing the same clothes in which he was arrested.

Accent? What Accent?

Being from New York had some advantages and disadvantages, especially working in Texas. One of the advantages was having an accent that was unique and could be used in your favor.

One time we were trying to get an interview from a guy we just arrested. He didn't waive his rights, but the agent talking to him was having a problem getting him to talk.

"Let me try," I said.

I talked to the agent about the suspect's background and learned he had a New York connection. He also briefed me on the investigation and other detailed information.

"Go tell the suspect that I'm an agent sent down from New York to assist on this investigation," I said, still hatching my plan inside my head.

While he went back to the interrogation room, I grabbed a bunch of blank papers and stuffed them into a folder. Entering the room, the agent introduced the suspect to me.

"This is some file you have," I said, totally faking it. "I'd like to talk with you about your role in this investigation. I understand you're quite the entrepreneur—buying guns here in Texas and then sending them up to New York."

Sitting down, I took the papers out of the folder and acted as if I was reviewing them. I asked the suspect a question and after each of his answers I would look at the papers as though I was validating his statement.

After a few minutes of this he gave us a complete confession. I guess he bought the entire story. The accent? Well, that was the real thing.

Surveillance Is So Glamorous

ATF participated in a program called the International Traffic in Arms Regulations or ITAR. It's a set of U.S. government regulations that control the export and import of defense-related articles and services on the United States Munitions List. Essentially, it was developed as a way to identify people who were trying to illegally import guns into Mexico. This was harder than you might think, given the proliferation of firearms in Texas.

On rare occasions, we received information from an FFL, or Federal Firearms Licensee, the people who sell firearms out of storefronts.

One time, we received information that an individual was taking a van full of firearms down to Mexico. Carl gathered eight agents in the office and instructed us to sit on the suspect's house and wait for the van to leave.

It was late spring 1990 and just starting to get hot during the day. I was partnered with a senior agent named Nick. We were told this would be a short surveillance, and that it would start as soon as the van left the subject's house. Then we would pass the van off to other officers down the state until they arrived at the Mexican border. As they were attempting to cross the border and leave the United States, that's when ATF would stop them.

The crazy thing was, U.S. Customs had to make the arrest. U.S. Customs has authority when a suspect attempts to exit the United States. Up to this point, ATF didn't have enough to get a warrant. Still, I thought it was just crazy that we were doing all this work and not arresting the bad guys ourselves.

Nick and I joined the others in the morning. We were sitting in his car and, of course, you can't sit there and run your engine all day to keep the air conditioning on. You had to shut the car off for short breaks and just sit there with the windows open, baking in the Texas heat.

Things weren't going according to plan and when night fell, we were still waiting. Then Carl and Don decided to get a motel room so we could take shifts getting rest, using the bathroom and washing up. You'll be shocked to learn that I never saw that motel room—it was used almost exclusively by Carl.

Nick and I sat in the car waiting, waiting, waiting and grabbing short naps when we could. We needed to be cautious, as we were not in one of Houston's better neighborhoods. We were still in the car as 24 hours passed; 30 hours passed; 40 hours passed.... We were at the 47-hour mark in the surveillance when Carl finally asked over the radio, if anybody wanted a break.

We should have been getting breaks all along.

"You want a break?" Nick asked me.

"Sure," I said.

It took roughly 40 more minutes until we got a call on the radio to say our relief was on the way. Then a few minutes later we got another radio call telling us that once we were relieved we could go home.

"What the hell are they talking about?" Nick asked me after hearing that. He jumped back on the radio for clarification.

"What's going on?" Nick asked the agent on the radio.

"Why are we being sent home?"

"You asked to be relieved," was the reply that came back across the radio.

"That's not what we were asked," Nick replied. "We were asked if we needed a break. We haven't been on break since the surveillance began."

We found out later they forgot to put us on the break rotation list, and never bothered to give out updates on the investigation. The surveillance team ended up leaving and about 12 hours later the subject finally took off for the Mexican border. At the border stop, Customs only recovered three small handguns. It was disappointing to us all.

A few months later I joined a second ITAR surveillance. The scenario was similar to the first one, although this time it was closer to summer and even hotter. I remember being so hot just sitting in the front seat of the car. I tried napping from time to time, and sleeping so hard that I drooled on myself.

I remember talking to Bob, the agent I was with, and saying how crazy this was. If we were in an accident or even involved in a shooting, we would have been put in jail due to the number of hours worked. The surveillance from start to finish lasted 72 hours.

Even the motel room situation was messed up again, although Carl must've gotten some crap from the last surveillance, because they did let a few other agents use it.

Bob and I followed the suspect from Houston, to McAllen, Texas. That's one long drive, but that didn't matter; all we cared about was getting closer to the end of the surveillance. Besides, the car was running and we were finally able to turn on the air conditioning. It was so hot outside; it felt like the earth was melting.

Now, when you're on a surveillance lasting as long as this one, a big issue is you are wearing the same clothes for the entire time, but it also means visiting some of the nastiest gas station bathrooms to take a G.I. shower.

A G.I. shower is taking some paper towels, wetting them, washing your face and then wiping your underarms. These restrooms were simply disgusting. The tiles on the walls were so covered with dirt; the entire bathroom was the same gray-brown color. The sinks and toilets looked like a science experiment that had gone totally wrong—you could only see a little bit of white porcelain around the base of the sink.

We coordinated again with Customs to assist in the arrest, and when we got down to the border we told them the lane in which the van was located. Customs stopped the van and we all jumped out of our cars and ran towards it.

We got the suspect and his entire family out of the vehicle and began searching. It was one of those customized vans with multiple compartments and hiding places behind veneer inside walls. We ended up removing one of the speakers and found five small firearms the suspect was trying to smuggle over the border. Eventually our management ended these surveillances, because they required too much ATF manpower for a Customs arrest.

Press Your Pants

More and more, I could not believe how much Carl was getting away with. Not only in his poor professional conduct, but his personal conduct as well. He would talk a big game, but let things fall through his hands. He was just a mess.

One time he tried to get me into trouble with the supervisor. I walked into Carl's office and he started to yell at me.

"Why aren't your pants pressed?" Carl hollered.

He was upset because my pants were wrinkled behind the knees and on the upper part of the hips below the belt—exactly the area where pants wrinkle when you sit down.

In Houston, the average humidity levels are around 90 percent. In my opinion, unless you're wearing steel pants, they'll always wrinkle.

"Follow me. We're going to see Don," he said.

So we walked into my alcoholic supervisor's office. This guy always looked worse for wear in the morning.

"DiBetta's appearance is unprofessional," Carl whined to Don. "Look at how his pants are wrinkled behind the knees and around the front of his pants."

"What are you talking about, Carl?" Don said standing up in front of us.

"His pants are less wrinkled than mine."

I just started laughing and went to my desk. This stupidity was just so tiresome and petty – it was all a control game.

Moving On

By the end of 1990, I was off training status and could not wait to get out of my group. Congress had just enacted new laws for dealing with individuals caught with a firearm who had a history of at least three violent felonies.

ATF called this the Achilles Program. The objective was to target violent felons in the worst section of each major city throughout the country. For example, if a person with three violent felonies was caught with a firearm, he or she was given a mandatory sentence of 15 years with no opportunity for parole or pardon. The law also addressed those dealing drugs with firearms. They would receive a minimum of five years, as well as whatever sentence was warranted for the drug charge.

The kicker in this program was the sentencing guidelines. If an individual was caught with a machine gun, it led to a 30-year mandatory sentence with no chance of parole or pardon. I jumped at the opportunity to be a part of Achilles, just to get away from this idiot of a training officer.

Carl had the nerve to call me and tell me what a good agent I was. He asked me to stay in the group and work with him. I told him, thanks, but I wanted to try a new group and left it at that. I was glad I got away.

Chapter 3

TALES FROM HOUSTON

The Ins and Outs of an Achilles Case

In terms of making arrests, this is probably the best time in my career. I was in the new Achilles group, I had a new supervisor and I was far away from my ex-training officer.

The Achilles group concentrated on Houston's Fifth Ward—the worst part of the city due to its record number of violent crimes. This place was so bad we would take our shotguns with us on regular interviews. One time, we were in someone's house doing an interview and a drive-by shooting occurred, three houses down. The way the noise traveled, we all hit the ground—it sounded that close.

I was told by a local police officer about a telephone repairman who was fixing a phone box on the street, when another man raped him. The patrolman went on to say the phone company went to the mayor wanting police protection whenever doing repairs in the Fifth Ward or they would cut off phone service. The mayor's office came back and told them they had to provide the phone service or the city would take action against them. That's how crazy it was in the Fifth Ward.

It was a shame, too, because the Fifth Ward was once a beautiful place with old, large Victorian homes, once exquisite, but now run-down. You could pick up one of these houses for less than $10,000, but the crime was so bad there were very few takers.

While I was working in the Achilles Program, I decided to target the three-time violent felony violators as opposed to the drug dealers. The first year I was in the Achilles group, I investigated six Achilles cases and they all ended with convictions. Each defendant received an average prison sentence of nearly 18 years without a chance for parole or pardon. I also processed a sawed-off shotgun case, as well as a drug dealer with a firearm case. To this day, I believe those six cases is still an ATF record for the three-time violent felony possession convictions in a year.

ATF, as a law enforcement agency, is at an interesting and *strange* place in the law enforcement community. I always equated us to salesmen. As a result of state laws overlapping with federal laws, we had to sell our services to local law enforcement as well as the U.S. attorney's office.

Just about every federal firearms law, with the exception of those regulating federal firearms licensees, has a sister law on the state books. So, when the state would arrest somebody, they had the option of either taking them to state court or getting us involved and taking it to federal court.

It's not that we didn't initiate our own cases, but we worked hand-in-hand with state and local law enforcement in seeing that the strongest case, and most time served, be sought against an individual committing a crime. For the most part we would prosecute the case due to our mandatory sentences.

One way in which I regularly worked and got to know local law enforcement was by helping them on search warrants. We called this "help digging." I tried to work with the major crime unit in the Fifth Ward. When I introduced myself, I told them if they needed any assistance, especially during warrants, I was more than happy to help.

Many of these local law enforcement investigators have a lot of experience dealing with federal agents. How you handled yourself while assisting them in processing a crime scene was often the difference between getting asked back to assist or not. We've all seen the people who hold up the shovel and don't do anything else all day! This was why many federal agents never get called back. I always got called back.

I made every effort to help the local LEOs better document and process evidence. I did this for two reasons. One, I did not want a case thrown out due to poorly processed evidence. The second reason was selfish on my part. If I was handed a federal case, I didn't want to deal with one that was screwed up.

One of my most memorable investigations began when I received a call from a Houston police investigator. He told me they just arrested one of the most active criminals in the area. Ray was involved in extortion, attempted murder, murder, drug dealing, robbery, burglary, and car theft. You name it, this guy was involved in it.

Ray was a 24-year old with a record of more than 20 arrests, including four violent felonies. He had been sentenced to well over 30 years for the crimes he committed. But like I mentioned before, Texas convicts were only serving 28 days for every year they were sentenced. So, he'd only served about three years in prison.

The arresting officers told me that Ray was with two of his friends at the time of his arrest. In their vehicle they had a loaded SKS, which is a civilian semiautomatic rifle that looks like an AK-47. Each suspect also had a handgun on them, and there were hooded masks and extra ammunition in the glove box.

The officer also shared that Ray was going for the rifle when they confronted him, but stopped when the officer shouted at him. The officer thought he was definitely going to be in a shootout.

The second person in the car, Jim, was sitting in the front seat on the passenger side. He had one felony conviction with several other arrests on his record. The third guy, Tyrone, didn't have a felony conviction; therefore, I couldn't put federal charges on him. He went to the state for trial where he was charged and released on bond. Just to cover our bases in case something went wrong in federal court, the other two individuals were also taken to state court, arraigned and released on bond.

In most cases they were back on the streets long before we had all the reports written.

Making the Arrest

So I indicted Ray and Jim on federal charges, and got arrest warrants for both. My main target was Ray. I ended up arresting him when he appeared for his court date on state charges, and for Jim, I sent a team to arrest him earlier that same morning.

I transported Ray to the federal courthouse in Houston. I could tell by his face, body expressions, and the subconscious noises he was making that he was highly upset and agitated by the time we arrived. My partner had to go park the car, so I walked him through one gated parking lot and into the building through a buzzer-controlled door by myself.

As I led Ray into the parking lot, I could feel him trying to flex the muscles in his upper arm. He was also mumbling a few words I could not make out. He was handcuffed behind his back and usually when somebody acts this way, they are thinking about trying to get away. You want their muscles to be relaxed and not ready to fight.

We entered the building and were buzzed into the Marshal's elevator. I turned him around and had him face the corner before I pressed the button of floor I needed. I didn't want him to see exactly where we were going in case he made a break for it.

On the elevator ride he started to mumble again. We left the elevator and were buzzed through another door into a hallway leading to the processing room, where we were once again buzzed in. After entering the processing room, I had to immediately go into a caged area where there was a gun locker for my weapon.

I was getting a little nervous. So far I hadn't seen another human being since my partner dropped me off in the parking lot, my prisoner was highly agitated and I needed to lock up my gun.

"Everything all right?" I asked Ray as I sat him on a bench in the processing room.

"Yes," he replied in a clearly hostile tone.

"Keep your eyes looking straight ahead while I remove your cuffs."

I figured if he was going to do anything, it was going to be now. After I removed his cuffs, I put them in my hand with the shank at the base of my palm and the cuffs over my knuckles, like you would if you had on a pair of brass knuckles.

I guess he saw my hand, because he calmed down a little bit and did not give me any more trouble during the processing. A few minutes later, I was relieved to finally see my first Marshal.

The second defendant, Jim, had just one felony conviction and was arrested with a gun under his pillow. He decided he wanted to cooperate. In the federal system, and in some states, they have what is called a "proffer." This is when the defense attorney, the assistant U.S. attorney and the investigative agent talk to the defendant to see what information they want to surrender to help reduce their sentencing. The U.S. attorney's office calls this a downward departure from the federal sentencing guidelines.

So the assistant U.S. attorney (AUSA) on this case, Paul, called a meeting. About six other AUSA's joined us. They were there to watch me interview this defendant.

I suppose I was developing a reputation for getting some pretty good interviews from defendants as well as witnesses. I told Paul, the AUSA, I didn't think it was a good idea to set up the interview this way. Even though Jim was willing to give up information, when there's an audience of six AUSA's around, people feel uncomfortable. It's like speaking in front of a crowded room.

Anyway, I began the interview, and as always I asked Jim some basic pedigree information and talked to him a little bit about whom he hung out with. Then I showed him pictures of the people he was arrested with—he identified them. I asked him what car they were in and what time of day it was when the police stopped them.

"What happened the night you were arrested?" I asked him.

"We were drinking, got into our car and then the police stopped us," was his simple reply.

"What happened when the police arrested you?"

"The police yelled at us to get out of the car and get on the ground."

"How long have you known Ray?"

"Over 10 years."

"Do you spend a lot of time driving around with Ray?"

"Yeah, all the time."

"Why did you guys have all of those firearms?"

"We need them to protect ourselves in this neighborhood."

"Well, why did you have that mask and all those extra rounds of ammunition in the glove box?"

"I didn't know anything about that."

"Okay. What about the rifle on the backseat of the car?" I asked, showing him a photograph of the firearm lying in the car.

"I never saw that gun before."

You didn't have to be a rocket scientist to figure out that this guy was not giving us any information.

"This guy is useless," I said to his defense attorney. "So far he has given us no information. Do you want to talk to him before we go any farther?"

They whispered to each other and indicated they wanted to continue.

"Do you want to add anything to the questions I asked you earlier?"

"No."

This is a waste of time, I thought as I readied my final question.

"What was said in the car as the police officers pulled you over?"

"What do you mean?"

"When the police were pulling you over did you say... just hide the drugs? Throw the weed out of the window? We are going to shoot this officer? Where's the registration? What was said?"

"Nothing."

"I do not consider this in any way shape or form cooperation, and this is a waste of our time," I said to the defense attorney.

Looking back at Jim, I asked, "Are there any other crimes or other information you want to share with us at this time?"

"No."

Jim was pretty much a dead end.

Believe it or not, Tyrone, the guy with no previous record, was the most interesting case. After he was out on bond from this arrest, he and another individual tried to rob a Colombian drug dealer.

The story I heard was they broke into the dealer's apartment, thinking it was unoccupied, and got into a gunfight. The person Tyrone was with took a bullet to his head. The medical report said it was like getting a frontal lobotomy. He survived, but became totally incapacitated.

Tyrone shot his way out of the apartment. I don't recall exactly how, but he was identified and the police went back for him. They found him trying to hide on his roof. When I went to interview him in jail, I received permission from his defense lawyer to talk with him about anything but the current case in which he was involved.

I knew the Harris County Sheriff's office Intel unit that worked out of the prison. I asked if I could interview Tyrone in their office. They told me that as an enticement I could give him a cigarette and one phone call. I then asked them about the possibility of moving him to a different cellblock and they said it was fine so long as it was within reason.

I went to the interview with a deputy, and I let him have a cigarette. Then the three of us talked for a while.

"You know you really screwed up by going after a Colombian drug dealer. That's a tight knit group in this community, and usually the people who mess with them end up with a Colombian necktie," I said to him looking for any kind of reaction.

A Colombian necktie is having your throat cut and your tongue pulled down through your lower jaw. Really unpleasant business.

You could tell by the expression on his face he was a little taken back by that.

"You know, if you feel endangered and cooperate, we could move you into a different cell block."

Tyrone just gave me a blank stare.

"Because I'm such a nice guy," I said, "if you cooperate you can have one phone call right out of this office when we we're done."

He quietly agreed to talk to us and said, "Before we went to the club we were doing street robberies and protecting our drug turf."

"Who was your leader?" I asked.

"Ray."

Tyrone went on to say they left their guns in the cab of the car because the club had metal detectors. He also confirmed to me that Ray pretty much ran a large part of the Fifth Ward.

"You realize when you testify, you will be asked about your criminal past and current charges?" I asked him.

"Yes."

"When they ask you, just remember in this country you're innocent till proven guilty."

From across the table he started to nod his head in agreement and said, "That's right."

"You will also be asked if we offered you any cash rewards or anything for your testimony. Just tell the truth and understand we are not offering you anything on your current charges because your lawyer told us 'not to talk to about that subject.'"

"By the way, do you repair roofs?"

"Why do you want to know that?" I could see the puzzled look on his face as he stared back at me.

"Well, because the police arrested you on the roof." This elicited a quick laugh. After over an hour interview it was good to leave it on a light note. Tyrone had his cigarette, made a quick call to a girlfriend who did not want to talk to him and went back to his cell.

The U.S. attorney was amazed. He told me it made his case a lot easier to prosecute.

Heading to Trial

In your career, nothing takes precedence over a trial. That is your number one priority. In this case, the trial preparation took only a couple of days. I went so far as to go to a used car dealership to take photographs of a vehicle that was the same year, make and model of the one involved in the case. I even removed the backseat to show there was no way the defendant could have hidden the gun in such a location.

The best part about these cases was that the trial typically lasted one day. In this instance there were three parts to our case:

Determining each individual's prior criminal history. That was easily proven with finger print comparisons.

Demonstrating an interstate nexus. The recovered firearms were researched to determine where they were manufactured to show they did cross state lines.

Proving the actual possession of a firearm. Was a firearm possessed at the time the defendant was arrested?

There was usually a suppression hearing on all evidence recovered from the arrest; if you win the suppression hearing, that means all the evidence is admissible in court.

Once you have those three parts of your case and you meet that burden of proof, you get a conviction. The only thing the defense can really attack is the possession of the evidence in the case. Even if the defense loses the suppression hearing, the prosecution still had to show they possessed the firearm.

Cases usually followed the same timeline. At nine o'clock a jury would be picked; 10 o'clock the case would start; by lunchtime the prosecution would rest; by about four o'clock the defense rested; and then closing statements were made. The jury would adjourn, and about 5:30 the verdict would be read.

The longest part of the trial was usually when I got on the stand. I don't know if the defense team was trying to get their money's worth, or if they just enjoyed it, but I was usually on the stand for about two hours. It wasn't because I didn't have command of the facts, or could not answer the questions; they were just trying to probe to see if there were any weaknesses in the case. I expected this and was always well prepared.

This case was no different, except this time the defense attorney was a paid lawyer and not a public defender. I had never gone up against this attorney and I was not sure of his style. But as soon as I saw him cross-examine a few of the witnesses ahead of me, I understood his technique.

He's what's called a "muddy-the-waters lawyer." He would try to take whatever was said and twist it around in an attempt to confuse the witness.

Once I took the stand, things followed their normal course. First, the prosecution asked about my skills and abilities as an ATF agent.

Next they discussed the details of the investigation—what happened? What was my role? What actions I took?

It's been my experience that the nicer the defense lawyer was in greeting you, the more of a beating he was going to try and put you through while on the stand.

"Good morning, Agent DiBetta. How are you doing on this beautiful day?"

Oh crap. Here it comes.

When sitting on the witness stand, the defense attorney is to the right as you look out onto the gallery, and the jury is to the left. The witness is usually sitting on the left side of the room with the judge to the right. When testifying, I was told to always address the jury directly when answering questions.

Well, he started asking me all kinds of questions—everything from how long I lived in Texas to what I thought of the weather. I was having none of it and replied with short, concise answers. I knew I was getting to him, because he was getting angrier and angrier while asking questions.

"Why didn't you whittle a gun and try to put it under the seat?" He asked me at one point.

"I don't whittle," I said, generating loud laughter throughout the courtroom.

Next, he tried to trip me up on photos that were taken. I asked for the photos and showed the jury each one was date stamped.

He continued to ask me over and over: "Was the gun under the backseat" (not accessible to Ray)? I replied, "No, the gun could not be under the backseat because of the vehicle's seat design." It did not allow space enough for anything, let alone a gun.

He asked again and I said, "Not without the seat sticking up and damaging the firearm." I raised my arm to show how the seat would be in an unnatural position. He then asked the same question over again. Finally, I said, "Judge, the answer is no." I didn't say anything else, but I still raised my arm to show how the seat would not fit properly had there been a firearm placed underneath it.

He became so frustrated with me that he spat out six questions in rapid fire.

"Would you please repeat each question, slower, and one at a time?" I responded.

At that, he got so flustered he said, "No further questions," then sat down without getting answers to any of his questions.

For me, the best part of this trial was when Tyrone got on the stand. After he testified about the events of that day and answered all of the prosecutor's questions, it was the defense attorney's turn.

The first thing he did was to go after Tyrone's criminal history. You should've seen the look on the defense attorney's face when Tyrone responded with, "I am innocent till proven guilty" after the first charges were read to him.

That attorney went through five pending charges and each time Tyrone said, "I am innocent till proven guilty." This infuriated the defense attorney.

"Did the prosecution offer you anything in exchange for this testimony?" he asked Tyrone.

"No."

"What did the agent instruct you to say while you are on the stand?"

"I was told to just tell the truth."

"What did he tell you to say?"

"Just tell the truth."

And with that he said, "No further questions" and just sat down. The trial ended before five o'clock.

The prosecution rebuttal showed all the pictures again, highlighting all the time stamps.

The most exciting part of this case came at the sentencing. Ray, my real target in the case, was sentenced to 18 1/2 years without the possibility of parole or pardon.

In this courtroom, the defense and prosecution face each other and the judge was in the middle, back against the wall. I could see Ray was talking to his defense attorney after his sentence was read. He shook his head "no" when Ray stopped talking.

At that, Ray slammed his hands down on the desk and yelled, "This is bull crap!"

Ray then looked straight at me as I made a gesture towards him. This caused him to become so irate he threw the defense table over. I stood up and walked away as the Marshals jumped on him and subdued him.

After that, they had a tendency to assign extra marshals to my cases, calling it "The DiBetta Rule." When some of the Marshals would see me, instead of saying, "Hello," they would say, "The DiBetta Rule." It still makes me chuckle. One of my proudest moments, though, was walking back into that police station, and having the officers try to lift me up in celebration. It wasn't so much as to praise me, but to celebrate taking down one of the worst crews in the Fifth Ward.

Moving on to the SRT

It always amazed me how people were selected for things. Most of the time in ATF it was being in the right place at the right time, and my selection for the Houston Special Response Team (SRT) was no exception.

With the Achilles program in full swing and the increasing emphasis on gun violence, we were asked to do more difficult entries than our training had prepared us to do. So ATF decided to develop an SRT team in each of their divisions. At the time, it was an assignment you were invited to join rather than one for which you could volunteer.

I remember I was exiting the office building on my way to court, when my boss stopped me and briefly mentioned SRT. Since I was really busy with work and my personal life, I told him I was not very interested.

The next day I was out doing interviews when I received a page from the office. I remember being in a crappy part of town. At the time, we had no cell phones and payphones were everywhere, so I pulled over to get to the phone and return the page.

This is a vivid memory, because the phone I picked was pretty disgusting. The earpiece had stuff all over it and I remember wiping it on my pants. I called the office and talked to my supervisor, Ben. He told me I'd been selected for the SRT team.

"Thanks, Ben, but I'm really not interested at this time," I said in a frustrated tone.

"Your training starts on Monday," was his reply.

And that's how my SRT career started. Ben was also our team leader!

It was fun being on the SRT team. There was much more tactics training and far more firearms training. Most of the time as agents, when we had to qualify we shot at stagnant targets. As an SRT member, we shot once a month and we fired at all kinds of moving targets. Skeet shooting with our short barrel tactical shotguns was my favorite and because of the short barrel having such a widespread pattern, you had to get on target quickly.

But the assignment included a lot more work, too. I remember starting at six in the morning just to serve someone else's warrant, because our practice was to do arrest and search warrants together. We also had to help search the house. Then after that, you'd start your day and, depending on the schedule, you might also have to serve another warrant later on.

Depending on what we were doing, we'd physically carry a lot of equipment on our person. You never knew what type of entry you were going to encounter. We did everything from fortified houses to house trailers. Over the years, we went over tall brick walls and had to break down fortified entryways. We were targeting experienced criminals who rarely made our work easy. It was not at all like TV. Sometimes it took quite a while to get into some of the houses.

By the end of four years, I'd participated in well over 250 high-risk warrants. When I say high-risk warrants, we were not just walking up to the door and handing someone a piece of paper. For these warrants we were in full gear, breaking down the door and having up to 16 agents making entry. All the criminals we went after had felony convictions, and many of them had multiple felonies. Just about all of them had some kind of firearm; after all, we were ATF. After each of these warrants we were glad no one was hurt. We were always happy to go home.

Houston was hot. I mean really hot and humid. The city was built on a swamp, and there were times in the summer when you looked out the window and could actually see the waves of heat rolling across the parking lot. It's a wonder the roads didn't melt.

As part of this new program, ATF bought us a vehicle—a box truck we called a bread truck. The truck had two air conditioning units. One unit was at the front of the truck, and the second one was the smallest roof mounted air conditioning unit you ever saw in your life. I think the person who purchased these vehicles had no idea how hot it got in Houston and in the back of this truck!

One time we took it to get serviced and asked if the air-conditioning unit was appropriate for an area the size of the back of the truck. I remember the man laughing at us and saying, "Well, down here in Texas we would have three of those units on there."

The bread truck was a simple design; it had two benches down the side, storage underneath those benches and storage along the sides of the walls. There were 16 members to our team, and between 12 and 14 of us were used to serve each warrant.

In law enforcement it seems as if you're always waiting for something or someone to show up, or for a deal to be completed. Being an SRT member was no exception. I remember waiting for hours, sitting in the back of this truck shoulder to shoulder, with all our gear on, waiting for the "go" signal. We'd have the air conditioning on and the doors open and it still felt like we were in an oven and going to melt!

Whenever possible, we would try to sit in our cars as long as we could before getting into the bread truck. Our vest and helmet always smelled of sweat, no matter how much you tried to clean it. Ugh! But at least your sweat smelled better than the beans!

In Texas they love their beans. There would be agents who would eat beans the night before, and play a game in which they wanted us to guess the type of bean they ate based on the odor of his flatulence. It was so gross, but I guess it helped pass the time!

Some Intensive Training and Impressive Shooting

My first formal training, other than monthly shooting and basic tactics training with the SRT group, was with the Harris County Sheriff's Department in Texas. Our SRT training was not as intense as the formal training we received from the sheriff's department. At the time, ATF did not have formal training for SRT members; it was in the development process at headquarters. As a result, we were sent to different local training classes.

The Sheriff's course was a two-week class, which had heavy emphasis on tactics and shooting. It was a lot of fun, was very physical, and there was plenty of shooting. During one of the exercises you were given 10 bullets, and had to climb on 10 obstacles while firing your weapon. The course required us to hang upside down, scoot up ladders, and suspend ourselves from a cement tube that was off the ground—stuff like that. You were not allowed to pass the obstacle until you hit the target. I went 10 for 10 and was class champion. For my prize, I got to watch everybody else do push-ups.

Next was a speed shot competition, where two people stand side-by-side and tried to shoot targets that swung from side to side. The person with the fewest number of targets remaining on his side would win. As my class battled, the final two were me and another

ATF agent. He beat me by one shot and then he enjoyed watching the rest of us do push-ups.

Every morning the instructors would conduct a firearm inspection. Our firearms were different from the local police at the time and they were a lot easier to clean. Another ATF agent and I were accused of using new firearms each day because our weapons were so clean. We both laughed about that.

During the summer of 1992, ATF sent about half of its SRT teams through a newly developed training course at beautiful Fort McClellan, Alabama. It was the same place I did my basic training and advanced school when I was in the Army's military police. The fort was being shut down, and now the military was trying to use it for other activities. It was a home to the military police and had a huge mount site, which is basically a fake city used to practice urban fighting. It was August and brutally hot, but being from Houston, at least we were used to it.

We were there with a team from Detroit. Fortunately, our team leaders were more realistic about training than those heading the Detroit team. For example, the Detroit leaders wanted the team to run from the barracks to the gym to do morning PT (Physical Training), then run back, take showers and be ready for the day's training. While the Detroit team did this, our team leaders refused and had us take the van back and forth to PT.

Still, this did not eliminate the dangers of heat exhaustion during training. I remember sitting on our bunks across from a team member while getting ready for lunch, when suddenly he started talking to me. I realized he was not even speaking a language. He was just talking gibberish. I called for another agent and we picked him up and threw him into a cool shower.

The medics came and he was taken off training for the rest of the day. I was thinking to myself, that's all it takes to get a day off of training? I could talk some gibberish!

During one of our training exercises, we practiced a spider hang. This is an extremely difficult maneuver designed to enable an officer to look into a window with limited exposure. We did this exercise with our vests and helmets on, but I could not imagine doing it fully weighed down with all our equipment. One of our team leaders, an older guy, tried this and he actually fell and hit the ground hard—knocking him out.

The medics immediately checked him out. There was no blood in his eyes or in his ears, and as they gave him the smelling salt, I yelled, "Check his pockets, check his pockets."

"What are you saying?" one of the medics asked.

"Check his pockets."

"Why?"

"To see if he has any money," I said with a laugh.

"Get the hell out of here," he hollered with a chuckle.

Once they gave the poor guy the smelling salts, he stood up a little shaken, but otherwise fine. He also got the rest of the day off.

One of the things that I found impressive during this training was we fired well over 2,000 rounds from our Sig Sauer handguns and did not have a single jam. Throughout the training they told us not to clean our firearms, so we could practice doing misfire drills; they wanted us to practice these drills while we were doing other exercises. The problem was, we had no misfires. It was amazing to see how well the weapons performed through all the challenges of dirt, sand and water.

When the training was over, our team felt pretty good. We were much smoother in clearing buildings and communicating using non-verbal signals. Believe me, after this training, if you weren't a better shot, you weren't going to get better.

BDUs and Naked Women

When we came back from training, it seemed there was more work to do than ever before. Some weeks we were doing four to five entries. You almost wanted to wear your BDUs (Battle Dress Uniform) to work because nine times out of ten, when you arrived you had to change into them.

There was one agent who everybody wanted to partner with on the bunker. The bunker was a ballistic shield carried by one agent who was in the lead and followed by another agent who carried his firearm on the opposite side of the bunker partner. For example, if you are right-handed, you would carry the bunker in your left hand and your firearm in your right, while your partner would carry his firearm in his left hand. But, the reason everybody wanted to partner up with this particular agent was his track record. Just about every time he entered a bedroom, he would find a naked or partially clad woman!

On one occasion, we were clearing a small house and as we made entry to clear each room, this agent's team and my team entered a bedroom. As you can imagine, an attractive and very pregnant women was in the bed. She was surprised and from underneath her pillow she pulled out a small, semiautomatic, pink-handled pistol and pointed it directly at me.

When someone points a gun at you, it always seems bigger than it actually is, but I felt comfortable enough behind the bunker that I did not have to shoot her, and I'm glad I didn't. Can you imagine the controversy of an agent shooting a pregnant woman? It would be unimaginable. She started shaking when we yelled, "Police! Put down the gun." She hesitated for a second, but then dropped the gun and started crying hysterically. Just think of the ribbing I would have gotten, if I'd been shot by a pink-handled gun.

This and That

For some reason, people in law enforcement like to get positive media coverage. As a result, some genius thought it would be a good idea to bring news crews with us as we made entry into houses while serving arrest and search warrants.

The first time the media was with my unit, we were serving a warrant on a crack house. As we were making entry, an agent dropped his firearm and when he tried to pick it up, he ending up kicking it further away towards the front of the door!

We finally made entry and found several crack cocaine cookies. They were called cookies because once the cocaine dried in the beaker it formed into the shape of a cookie. Anyway, lucky for us, the news media never used the footage of the agent dropping his gun. They were nice enough, however, to send us a copy of the incident, which we used to rib the agent whenever we could.

Some of the places we entered were pretty disgusting. I'm not just talking about a little dirt or clothing thrown around, I mean downright nasty. One of the worst places we entered was a shotgun shack in Houston.

"Why do they call these places shotgun shacks?" I asked a local police officer.

"It's because if you take a shotgun and shoot at the front door, you would clear the whole house," he said without thinking.

At this particular place, people were literally locked into the house to sell drugs. At the end of the day, if they did not have the amount of money the dealer expected, it meant they hadn't sold enough drugs and they would get seriously beaten.

We made entry into the house and there was a closed door. I kicked the door open, and literally a wall of stink was behind it. They were using the bathtub as a toilet, there was no air-conditioning and very few windows were opened.

It was July and the temperature at times reached well over 100° for many consecutive days. The smell was unbelievable, and of all the things I have ever smelled in my life, that had to be the worst.

"You need to search that," I said to the new agent there to help us process the scene.

"Job or no job, I'll quit before I ever do that," the newbie replied.

We all shared a big laugh. To my knowledge, that bathtub, filled to the brim with human waste, was never searched.

Taking on a New Role

My career was going pretty well. I was making a lot of arrests; I was always in court. In the ATF at the time, agent grade levels could typically go as high as a GS 12, and it was very difficult to get a GS 13 position. So when one came open as a Tactical Operations Officer (TOO), I put in for it.

In Texas, only two agents in each division held this position, and across ATF, there were about 45 TOO agents. As a TOO, you were in charge of all the technical assets ATF used to gather evidence, like a wiretap, or a DNR (dial number recorder)—where telephone numbers, but no voice recordings are collected. The TOO's also did body wires (concealed transmitters hidden on the body), body recorders, alert transmitters, pinhole cameras and video transmitters. We also were involved with advanced photography, concealing devices and any other duties the division assigned.

We had vast experience with radio signals, and were proficient in the use of repeaters because of the limited strength of our transmitters. The repeaters were used to boost the signal to a higher strength giving us a greater standoff distance. We also worked with hidden video cameras and within eight months of being assigned as a TOO, we started using board cameras (the latest technology at the time). Board cameras are pinhole lenses mounted on a small circuit board measuring about two inches wide, four inches long and maybe less than ¼ inch thick.

It's not that I didn't like what I was doing in investigation, and I was very fortunate to have had some success at it, but I saw this as an opportunity to work on bigger investigations and learn some of the newest equipment and latest techniques being used in law enforcement. The pay increase was not too bad either, plus I remained on the Special Response Team (SRT).

Just to show you how consistent ATF management was, my supervisor, Ben, who I thought I got along with, begun bad mouthing me to another agent. This started no more than a week or so after I left his group to become the TOO.

"I thought you liked him and the work that he did?" the agent asked Ben.

"He left my group," was his response.

It was sad, sometimes, to see how petty people were in this agency. Instead of being happy for my promotion, he was mad because he lost a worker in his group.

The other TOO in my division, Frank, got the job about a year before, so we were both fairly new to the position. He was a good agent to work with, and he was meticulous in his bookkeeping and records.

As a TOO, you were under strict constraints when installing equipment for two reasons: limited access to where equipment needed to be placed and the limited range of the transmitters. I remember one of our first deals—a generic term for any interaction with a subject in an investigation, i.e. drug deal, gun deal—we were using an elementary school as a listening post and the equipment was not working. Frank and I went to the school to identify the problem and attempted to fix it.

Since Frank already attended some of the training schools required of us to perform this job, I was mainly there to observe and learn. He talked about the ABCs: Antennas, Batteries and Connections. He was having no luck solving the problem.

"Let me have the controls to the camera and I'll give it a try," I said to him.

I took the controls, pressed one button and everything started working! We both just laughed, and said, "FM" (f'ing magic, a term widely used to describe equipment that was previously not functioning and through no rational explanation started to function properly).

We never made fun of each other about any technical problems we experienced with the equipment. For example, one time my partner was working on some cameras and VCRs, and nothing was working. I checked everything while he continued to work. I could see the frustration in his face until I picked up the plug and tapped him on the shoulder with it. We both looked at each other and started laughing again. Sometimes you become so entrenched on particular pieces of equipment that you failed to see the big picture.

Prior to taking this job I had never heard the expression, "That's impossible, that cannot happen" so often in my life. One time when we were installing some DNR's, we had to hardwire them within a three-mile radius of the target's phone. The phone company called this "all copper," because there couldn't be any gaps or breaks in the connection between the DNR and the suspect's phone.

I was coming back from a road trip where I had removed three DNRs and was going to install one of them in another ATF office. I hooked up the bridge between the bad guy's phone line and our phone line at the telephone box, and then went back to the office to hook up the device that actually printed out the phone numbers.

While I was configuring the equipment, I found a problem. Once the machines were set up, if a problem occurred it would print out an error code. You were to then call the company and they would walk you through the problem you were experiencing.

So, I called the number and told them how I set up the equipment and gave them the code. Well, the first words out of his mouth were, "That's impossible, that cannot happen. You cannot be getting that code."

"That's the code the machine is giving me," I replied. "Why would I make up a code?"

"But, that's impossible, that cannot happen," he said again.

"Do you want me to fax you a copy of the print out code?"

"Yes, because this should not happen."

So I got off the phone with him, faxed the information and waited for his call. A few minutes later my phone rang.

"Well, I guess this can happen," he said with a tone of disbelief. "Do you have any more machines available?"

I used pieces from all three machines to build one working machine. I would have given this guy the business for making me fax him the code, but it was already a long trip. I knew I would need his assistance in the future, and I did.

A big technological advance was a new device called a RDNR, or remote dial number recorder. These were much easier to install and use. An agent could call them from anywhere and download the information onto a computer.

In this one instance we were way out in the country, we hung our equipment in the phone box, tested it and everything worked fine. A week later the phone company called us because our target was complaining that he was getting strange noises on his phone. We did some troubleshooting and the device indicated a battery problem. I reported this finding to the company representative and once again they said, "That's impossible. That cannot happen."

The company instructed us to switch out the device. We went back out to pull the equipment and discovered a bunch of fire ants inside. There were so many bugs they caused an arc on the two leads inside the equipment!

I called back to report what happened and again they said, "That's impossible. That cannot happen." We opened the equipment and the ants fell out onto the ground. They were dead from being electrocuted. Because the guy at the other end of the phone was such a jerk, I sent the equipment back to him, ants and all. He called me back a week later and apologized to me. He said he did not realize how these ants nested and were able to swarm.

I was a true believer in preparedness, especially when it came to doing deals. I would always try to have multiple recorders and as many cameras as I could when videotaping deals.

I used to love syncing the sound onto the video recorder from the cassette recorder. It was like making a movie. You have two people talking in the distance and you hear every word, as you watch the exchange. The best part was when the assistant U.S. attorney, the defense attorney, the defendant, the case agent and I would be in a room and the defendant would deny everything. The U.S. attorneys would ask the defendant if the story they told was the one they wanted to stick with. The defendant would answer "yes." The assistant U.S. attorney would then say, "Turn on the video," and you could see the defendant's face just drop. You didn't have to get past the first minute of the tape before the defendant would say, "Okay. What's your deal?" That was great.

The Pressure Builds

Although every role at ATF came with pressure, it increased exponentially when you became a TOO, because not only were you responsible for helping out on a case, but you also had the responsibility of collecting the evidence. Here's what I mean:

This was an era when we used 35mm film instead of digital cameras, so you had to wait until the film was developed to see if you got the picture. Part of the TOO job was making sure the film was loaded correctly, you had the proper lenses and everything was working. It had to be right and that was the reason for carrying multiple pieces of equipment as back up. And, as always, you did not want to be known as the guy who screwed up the investigation.

Phil, the Houston special agent in charge at the time, thought it was important to have good agents in the TOO position. Other divisions within ATF used this position as a dumping ground for agents who were not allowed to testify in court or were ineffective as street agents.

I cannot tell you how many times an investigation was saved by correcting evidence gathering failures or by telling other agents not to take shortcuts when processing the evidence. If the evidence was gathered incorrectly and/or marked improperly, it would kill the investigation and it would be thrown out in court.

Since I was still a member of the SRT, I was involved during the serving of warrants and the subsequent arrest in many investigations, especially the big ones. After we'd make entry into a house and cleared it, I would go to my car, take off my SRT gear, grab the video camera and a 35mm camera, and process the scene for evidence.

I recall one situation where after the warrant was served and arrest made, the case agent didn't want to do a pre-search warrant video—a video of the whole house before any searching is done. We shot the video anyway and a few weeks later the agent called and said the defendant was implying we planted a large amount of liquid cocaine in his house.

The only time I saw liquid cocaine was when I was working for U.S. Customs at JFK International Airport and someone tried to smuggle it in a wine bottle. It turns out this was the largest liquid cocaine seizure in the state of Texas up to that time. It certainly explains why the defendant was so adamant in claiming we had planted it there.

"Look at the pre-search video and identify the bottle located in the kitchen," I said to him.

"I'll take a look and call you right back," he said.

Sure enough, within 20 minutes my phone rang.

"I found the bottle in the video," he yelled excitedly. "I'll never doubt you again!"

That made me laugh, but I had made his case.

Another thing I tried to institute as a TOO was training. The only real training received on technical equipment was at the beginning of a career during your time at the Academy. So, if you were in the field for 15 years, most of the technical equipment on which you were trained was outdated.

I would go to each of the field offices and pull out their equipment and review it with the field agents in the office. On one occasion, I was conducting the training and an agent said, "You brought a lot of equipment with you today."

"This is all your equipment," I said. "It is assigned to this group and it was in your electronics locker."

He was stunned. It really wasn't his fault. Most of the time when a new piece of equipment came in, people just threw it into the equipment locker without even looking at it. The training exercises I coordinated increased the use of electronics in our division by well over 40 percent.

That pretty much sums up my four years as Houston Division TOO. It's not so much that I couldn't get the equipment to work or we failed to collect the evidence, but Murphy's Law always worked side-by-side with us.

Chapter 4

A PLACE CALLED WACO

My First Encounter with the Branch Davidians

It's amazing how so many things can change with just one phone call. In 1992 the Internet and e-mails were not commonly used. Most conversations were still done over the phone, not through e-mails or texting.

Our office received a call from the division office informing us of a compound outside Waco, Texas, at a place called Mount Carmel. We were told the people living there were converting firearms into automatic weapons, and UPS reported a large shipment of grenade simulators. The neighbors and others in the surrounding area could hear gunfire, some of which they believed to be automatic gunfire, as well as small explosions. The case agent at the time, Danny, was on a Secret Service detail, and our supervisor asked Frank and me to go to Waco and determine the feasibility of putting up a pole camera to monitor the activities of this group known as the Branch Davidians.

Frank and I attended our first meeting on July 30, 1992. We met with two lieutenants from the McLennan County Sheriff's Department at a vehicle repair shop in downtown Waco. They had been watching this group for a long time and had recently responded to a shooting at the compound between the Branch Davidians' two leaders—who were vying for power.

It's understood this is when David Koresh took over the site and became the leader of the Branch Davidian church in Mount Carmel. The police officers told us that no other federal agency wanted anything to do with this investigation. They knew the Davidians were conducting credit card and check fraud, but the Secret Service didn't want to get involved.

The sheriff's office became aware of some troubling behavior within the compound from Davidians who left the group and shared it with them. For example, they knew Koresh was nullifying marriages between couples that went to live at the compound, and he was the only one who could have sex with the females. If the couples living at the compound had any daughters, by the first menstrual cycle, Koresh would begin having sex with her. Texas protective services did not have enough evidence to do anything about it and had very limited access to the compound.

After Koresh took over the church, he wanted to construct one massive building where everybody lived, worked and prayed instead of several different houses aligned along a horseshoe-shaped driveway. As a way to save money in constructing his temple, Koresh started tearing down the smaller houses and reusing the wood.

Some of the houses that were torn down were more than 20 years old. There was no protection from the elements for the wood used to build the compound. It was dried out and I believe this fact played a major part when the compound burned down in 1993.

The lieutenant showed us aerial pictures of the new building's early construction. The pictures showed the Davidians were reinforcing the lower half of the exterior walls on the compound's first floor by applying additional layers of plywood to a height of about four feet. The officers also believed they filled the space between the two layers of plywood with either rocks or dirt.

Even though it was early in the investigation, it was clear to everyone that it was odd for Koresh to fortify his place in such a manner. The police also surmised his paranoia increased after he took over the church, and word was he believed he was fulfilling a prophecy.

ATF Begins Building its Case

It wasn't until October 2, 1992, that Frank and I installed the pole camera overlooking the compound at Mount Carmel. Very few poles were suitable for this operation, and our listening post was at the very limit of the microwave transmitter, which was 1 to 2 miles depending on the terrain. We were barely able to get any picture at all, but we believed it was worthwhile to try and get what we could through the device.

The following Monday, October 5, we met with Chuck and Donnie, the two ASACs (Assistant Special Agent in Charge—they were the number two men in the Division). Chuck was the ASAC in charge of the Field Offices outside the city of Houston, including the Austin group, which was responsible for the Waco area. Donnie was the ASAC of the groups (or offices within the Division city) within Houston city limits, as well as the TOO's.

In that meeting, Frank and I explained how big the compound was and even then we told them they had to see it to believe it. We also detailed some of the limitations we were having with the camera, but added that we were trying to get a different pole camera – one with a stronger transmitter for better picture quality.

We went to install the new camera on October 9, but had trouble with the camera inside our concealed shell. I had to go up in a bucket truck, also known as a cherry picker, and repair it. While I was up there, I was within a foot of a power line carrying more than 27,000 volts of electricity on the line. It had an orange protective cover on it, but it still made the hair on the back of my head stand up.

Suddenly we heard shots coming from the compound. I was still in the cherry picker and still worried about becoming toast, but I quickly grabbed my radio and called my partner.

"Can you see what location they are shooting from?" I asked excitedly.

"No, but it sounds like shotguns to me," Frank said.

Shotguns would never have the range to reach me up in that bucket, so I kept working. We finally got the camera operating properly. Because Austin was more than 100 miles from Waco, the case agent asked one of the police lieutenants who lived in the Waco area to go to the listening post once a day to replace the tape. After a while he began reviewing the tapes.

One day the tapes showed two planes landing behind the compound. The lieutenant noticed they were different planes because of the wing configuration, but he did not have the ability to get the tail numbers. We could have done that in our shop with the equipment we had or could have sent the tapes to other federal agencies to enhance the video and pull up those two tail numbers, but it wasn't done. The significance of this will become clear a little bit later.

My TOO partner, Frank, reminded me of a story about the electrician who helped us install the pole cameras and worked on the lines. During the Christmas of '92, the electrician tried to talk about the case at a Christmas party with a local police lieutenant who also was working with us. The lieutenant called me the next day. I called the electrician and read him the riot act. After I got off the phone with the electrician, Frank said to me, "I'll bet he was in tears over what he did." You're beginning to see how this case was going.

Unfortunately, it would get far, far worse.

Ratcheting Up Our Surveillance

On December 12, Chuck asked us to do a site survey for surveillance from the proposed undercover (U/C) house near the compound. This would allow us to get the latest intelligence and possibly document any firearms violations. The U/C house was a small, two-bedroom property about 600 yards across from the compound, with no trees around it. As you faced the house from the road, to the right was another small house where one of the Davidians, who was not as devoted to Koresh, was living. We also knew the house we were going to take over had been previously occupied by Davidians, but they had moved out several months earlier.

On December 18, there was a Waco planning meeting at the Houston field division office that turned into a tactical meeting. From what I recall from this meeting, there was very little talk about the actual investigation, but plenty of discussion of how we were going to execute a warrant on them.

I went to just about every one of these planning meetings, and some of the things said were good and some were not so good. Many ideas were floating around about how to effectively serve a warrant at such an isolated and large structure.

One of the team leaders, Bill, had the idea of the ATF doing a helicopter assault on the compound because of its remote location. The proposed plan called for a helicopter to land in front of the compound, some pyrotechnics were to go off to make it look like it was on fire and have other helicopters land as the Davidians gathered around the grounded helicopter to see what was going on. That's why our team went to helicopter training with U.S. Customs on December 17 at Hooks Airport, just outside of Houston.

By way of a little background, across ATF, the resident agent in charge is the supervisor for the group. The Austin, Texas group covered the Waco area. Their supervisor was confident and had a lot of common sense, but just as this case started, he resigned over misconduct in the office with another employee. Following ATF protocol, the group's most senior agent, Earl, was named the acting supervisor. I would encounter some interesting experiences with Earl in the coming weeks.

Our Special Agent in Charge (SAC) was a man named Phil. He worked in the Houston division for quite some time and was one of the better SACs I had in my career. He would always say, "The Houston division did a lot of good work but never received credit for it," and was always looking to showcase his division.

Earlier, I mentioned the two ASACs, Chuck and Donnie. Chuck arrived in Houston in 1992, having worked at headquarters in Washington, D.C., in our special operations division. He was credited with writing the plan for bringing multiple SRT teams together in an operation. Our work in Waco was going to operationalize his planning. Donnie was also fairly new to the position, having been recently promoted.

There was a lot of speculation among SAC Phil, ASAC Chuck and Bill, our team leader, about the successful execution of this warrant and how it would catapult all three of these officers into promotions. If you keep this in the back of your mind while we go through the story, it's my belief it will become a little clearer why things happened the way they did.

The holidays were here and Frank and I were told to prepare for surveillance from the U/C house. After the holidays, on January 5-6, 1993, we began the installation of a command post at a local community college to support the U/C house. The college was Texas State Technical College (TSTC), located just outside the city of Waco and fewer than 10 miles from the compound. During this trip we installed an antenna for a base station as well as six phone lines for this remote command center.

Frank and I were not part of the decision process for choosing who was to work in the U/C house. Initially, the ASACs were looking for people who could pass as college students, and they wanted to include some members from the Houston SRT team as well.

The ASAC Chuck, with the approval of the SAC Phil, decided to move eight agents into the small house and divided them into two teams. I called them the Austin group and the Houston group. There was no consideration made for whether or not these agents had any technical ability. In other words, the agents' interest, experience or aptitude in the use of our surveillance equipment was never a factor. That was made clear as the investigation wore on.

ATF Operations Commence

January 11 was the planned move-in date at the U/C house and the start of ATF's manned surveillance at the Mount Carmel compound. About a week prior to that we brought all the equipment destined for the U/C house to the Austin field office, so we could train the undercover agents on its proper use. It was clear from their lack of questions or enthusiasm that they had very little interest or aptitude in using the equipment.

Just like in any job, some people were better at things than others. Frank and I discussed this issue, and to help remedy the situation and eliminate any problems in assembling or configuring equipment, Frank labeled all the switches and knobs with letters and numbers prior to the move-in date. He wrote out exactly how to operate the equipment, left the owner's manuals with the gear, and took Polaroid pictures of each configuration.

Move-in day came as scheduled and as an added precaution, we did not have any of our equipment in the standard black Pelican cases. Instead, we put everything into unmarked brown boxes so nothing would appear unusual. Frank and I showed up when it was dark, giving us another level of concealment.

As we were moving in and setting up the equipment, Frank and I started to talk to the undercover agents about their cover story. Since they were trying to pose as college students, I told them TSTC was a technical college, and unlike a four-year college they might have tri-semesters, quarter semesters or the standard semester format. It depended on the major. I told them to pick a major and know the semester they were in. Sure enough, one of the Davidians' came by the next day and asked them those very questions.

We also suggested they have material mailed to them from the college on college stationery. We knew that one of the Davidians living in the compound worked for the Postal Service. Even though we knew the U/C house was not on his route, it was in such an isolated area and out of the way for the other rural carriers, that it was a wise precaution. We figured the Davidian letter carrier might tell the mailman of the U/C house that he would deliver the mail on his way home.

As we set up some of the high-powered lenses, we could see a scurry of activity among the Davidians. Many of them were outside moving stuff. I suggested to one of the undercover agents it could be they know something's going on here at your house or it could be their normal practice to work a lot in the evening hours when it was cooler.

Not long after, as Frank and I were setting up the equipment, I was shocked when two of the Austin agents said they were going to go work out and left the U/C house. We were both stunned by this. To me it reflected the level of commitment they had toward this operation.

Without giving away any trade secrets, some of the other equipment we had in the house included a long-distance lens with a night scope attachment on a small camera that connected to a VCR and monitor. We had the radio converter, which allowed you to place your handheld radio into an adapter. This boosted the power up to about 10 times what a normal handheld radio would transmit. We ended up putting the transmitting antenna in a small closet in the bedroom being used as a listening post. We put a metal sheet under the antenna, as it had better sensitivity in transmitting and receiving with a metal surface underneath of it.

We also had another high-powered lens attached to a video camera with an electric zoom, connected to its own monitors. On this unit we installed a video alarm. The video alarm allowed us to tell if the pixel count changed on a particular shot and would sound an alarm. You could also use it as a triggering device so a camera would begin recording if someone walked in the field-of-view at night.

"This alarm will prevent the Davidians from sneaking up on you," I said to an undercover agent in the room.

"I don't want that," he replied, surprising me. "It will keep me up at night."

We also had a 35mm camera with a high-powered lens able to shoot with night vision equipment. We also knew the Davidians had people with military experience, especially in communications. So we installed a broad-spectrum scanner to see if we could intercept any of their radio communications, knowing they used small hand-held radios. Our radio technician even flew over the compound to locate their antenna.

The U/C house was also equipped with an encrypted phone. This was operated with a key. We weren't sure if the Davidians were mirroring our phone lines—or splicing their phone wires into ours.

As far as the legal stuff goes, there was a more than 27-page affidavit written and approved by a judge in case the lenses from our cameras produced an image that broke the plane of the glass on the Davidians' compound—in other words, if you could see inside the house.

After that rocky start, it's not hard to believe things in the U/C house quickly started going downhill. The first issue was the schedule. The schedule was set up so that week one the Austin group worked day shift and Houston group worked the night shift and the next week they would alternate.

Well, the Austin group did not like how the schedule was written, so they changed it after the first week. Not satisfied with that change, they changed it again, resulting in the Austin group working days and Houston group working nights. This started the animosity in the house.

During this time, the U/C house let us know they could not do any night surveillance because the night vision did not work.

"What's the problem you're having," I asked an agent from Austin.

"The bright light from all the windows is bleeding over and blurring the entire picture," he said.

"That's called pluming," I told him. "That's actually a good thing. You can remove the night vision equipment. There is enough light to see what is going on without it."

We didn't hear anything from them for the next couple of days, until I was told by ASAC Chuck to call the U/C house and talk about the problems they were having with the 35mm camera.

I called the U/C house. We used a code word to activate the encrypted phones. The word was "pizza." When the agent at the house answered I said, "Hi. This is Dave. Do you want to go get some pizza?"

"No," he said, "we just had some pizza. Maybe when you come over we can get something else?"

"No. I'd really like to get some pizza and I feel like some pizza now," I said, becoming bewildered.

"No thanks. I don't want any pizza."

After a minute or so of this nonsense, I lost my composure. "Would you turn the f'ing key?" I screamed.

"Oh."

Once we were in the encryption mode, I reminded him about the code word and asked him what's going on with the cameras.

"The 35mm camera isn't working and I don't know what's wrong with it."

"Have you seen any pictures from it?" I asked.

"No."

"Frank and I will be up there tomorrow to see what's going on."

"Please don't bring Frank along," the agent pleaded. "He talks way over our head."

"Fine, I'll bring another agent along who recently used the equipment."

The agent I took with me the next day was Steve Willis. Steve was a fairly new agent who had just successfully used the equipment on a different operation. I got approval from ASAC Chuck and we headed up to the U/C house.

By now, ASAC Chuck knew there were problems up there. They just made a senior agent, Earl, who was about to retire, the acting supervisor and then assigned Don, another senior agent to run/supervise the U/C house. Another of the undercover agents, the one who met with the owner of the U/C house, had a baseball hat with the ranch's name on it. He took it upon himself to say that he was the team leader of the operation because he had the baseball hat, but no one listened to him. The whole thing was ridiculous.

A Long Day

Steve and I arrived at the U/C house to find only one agent in the house and he was playing a guitar. "Where is everybody?" I asked him.

"Out to lunch." I didn't know what to make of that and asked when would they be back.

About 20 minutes later they showed up and I asked them to explain the problem with the cameras.

"They don't work."

"Well, let me see some of the photos you've taken," I said.

"We don't have any."

"Okay, let me see your photo log."

"We aren't keeping one."

"Then how do you know the equipment isn't working?" I questioned.

"The case agent said the photos are no good," they replied.

"Fine. Show me what you're doing," I said.

"We don't know how to use the equipment," was the only reply.

Now, just as a reminder, they were there for almost two weeks and at this point they still didn't know how to use the equipment, it was their only purpose for being there!

I walked into the bedroom where the equipment was posted to try and figure out what was wrong. But all the equipment was shoved into a closet. I told them I would take one agent at a time and again review the proper use of the equipment.

I brought the first agent into the bedroom.

"Get the equipment out of the closet and set it up for me," I said.

He reached in and pulled out a tripod. He looked at the tripod and then looked at me. "How do you use it?"

I thought my head was going to explode. Anyway, I set up the equipment. The lens we were using was so big that it had an affixed f-stop. The only adjustments that needed to be made on the camera were to focus, adjust the shutter speed and then take the picture. After I repeated this to him several times he started to get annoyed with me.

Another of the U/C agents complained about focusing the camera enough to take a clear picture. So, I opened the backdoor of the U/C house and pointed the camera in the direction of an object so far that it could not be clearly seen with the naked eye.

"I don't see what you're pointing at," the agent said.

"That's the point. Look at how much power you have with this lens," I answered.

We went back into the surveillance room and I asked them, "How do you take a picture?"

"Through the glass and screen in the window," they said.

"That is part of your problem," I explained. "The glass sometimes polarizes or blurs the lens when you try to take a picture. All you have to do to prevent this from happening is open the window and take the picture."

"But it's too cold to have the window open," an agent whined.

I also noticed that they were taking pictures only with black and white film. When we set up the U/C house, we asked them to take one series of pictures of the compound in black and white to see if there were any antennas on their building.

We thought we could guesstimate the frequency of their radios by the size of the antenna they were using. But because the undercover agents were not paying attention to anything, they never changed the film; so all the pictures were in black and white, which made it more difficult to develop.

At the time we had to send out black and white film via overnight mail to our headquarters for processing. The black-and-white photos took up to 10 days to be developed. There was literally a small box full of exposed film that no one bothered to have developed. And that day all we heard was, "it's not my job."

After resolving all their equipment problems, I decided to take a series of photos with color film, have it developed and then show them the problems were resolved.

At the time the only way you could tell if a 35mm camera was getting the quality pictures you needed was to have the film developed. Steve and I drove more than 36 miles to have the photos processed at a camera shop in a small mall. There'd be no way of knowing the exact location of any of the pictures. But as an extra precaution, I also asked the photo lab worker to put the cover on the machine so he could not see the photos. I stood there while he was developing the photos.

In about an hour, I was looking at ID-quality photographs of heads and license plates. It was night by this time and we drove back to the U/C house to show the photos to the agents. When we arrived, the senior agent, Don, was there.

"You're going to blow this investigation, DiBetta," he yelled at me. "You had no right to get those photographs developed without informing me."

"I don't work for you and I went more than 36 miles from this place to get these photos developed. I used every precaution at the lab," I snarled back at him. "It's the only way to know for certain if a 35mm camera is working."

I showed him the photos and kept two to show ASAC Chuck back in Houston. I wasn't a "by-the-book" person, but because they were having so many problems I told them they had to have a photo log and they had to start developing the photos in a timelier manner.

"Dave, you're going to blow this investigation," one of the agents said to me. I'm thinking, *What now*? So I turned to him and asked, "Why?"

"Because you're wearing a wedding ring and a pager," he said.

My pager was black and was approximately 2"x4" and secured to my belt.

"First of all, if they can see me at night from their compound and notice while I'm walking that I have a wedding ring on or that I am wearing a pager, this operation is already blown."

You know when you sit in algebra class and think to yourself, "I will never use anything I am learning in this class." This day proved that thought wrong.

Don, the supervisor for the U/C house also wanted to move the listening post for the pole camera and have it repositioned inside the U/C house. I told him I would check it out. I got in my car and did a mileage distance from the pole camera to the house. I had two known sides and I could show that the distance from the transmitter to the proposed site inside the U/C house was too far. I didn't recall the formula name, but the math worked perfectly. We did not move the listening post.

Later that night when Steve and I were pulling out of the driveway of the U/C house, he turned to me and said, "I never heard so many people say, 'it's not my job.'"

"Yeah, they're killing me."

To this day I have never seen a photo that was taken by anyone in the U/C house.

More of the Same

The next day I showed ASAC Chuck the photos and told him what happened at the U/C house. I suggested he reduce the number of agents in the house and put Frank or me in to operate the equipment. I also told him about the night surveillance. I explained to him what they were doing wrong and what corrective actions were recommended.

I also suggested he talk to Steve about the things he saw at the U/C house. We talked a little more and then I left his office to go brief Frank on what he missed.

After talking to Frank and mulling it over for a couple of weeks, we were made aware of continuing issues at the U/C house. One night while looking at the compound, the undercover agents noticed one of the Davidians walking back and forth. He had something straight sticking up from his back and his hand was up by his chest clearly holding a strap.

If you've seen something such as that you would typically record that a sentry was walking back and forth in front of the compound in your surveillance report. The agents in the U/C house had a great debate over this because they could not see the whole rifle. This debate lasted for about a week. I believe they decided not to put this incident in the report. When I heard this, it kind of ticked me off because, you always error on the side of caution, and at the very minimum report that there appeared to be a sentry. This is how crazy the U/C house was.

Being made aware of stories such as this, I thought it would be best to talk to ASAC Chuck again. I figured he would be anxious to know things weren't going well at all.

In the 1980's, Chuck was in Miami serving on a task force on violent drug crime headed by then Vice President Bush. This was the time of the cocaine cowboys, and Chuck shared with us that he was there when the supervisor pressured an agent named Ariel Rios to do an undercover deal that clearly had all the warning flags up. Rios was later killed during his undercover drug deal. Chuck kept a photo of Ariel Rios in his office.

I went in to talk to ASAC Chuck about the investigation and how all these red flags were coming up. Again, I told him about the problems in the U/C house and how I believed there were too many people. I even mentioned Rios' name and said they never should have done his deal with all the problems with that investigation. Chuck went on to say, "I understand your concerns, but this is good training for these agents." So, we left it at that. I later thought this showed the investigation was not important. It was never about the investigation, it was about serving the warrant.

I then talked to ASAC Donnie, who was my direct supervisor, and shared with him all the problems we were having at the U/C house. He told Frank and me the investigation was not his area and everything had to go through Chuck. We tried to have him be an advocate for us and help make this a better case, but he would not have any part of it.

SAC Phil would regularly talk to us in our office. The next time I saw him I mentioned the problems we were having with the investigation and some of the solutions we already suggested. He looked at us and then started to go into a story about a time when he was in Chicago and he put a camera in a tree with a long cord to take pictures. His non-relevant story over, he left our office.

The lack of concern from the ASACs, and now the SAC, made it more apparent to Frank and me that neither the U/C house nor the intelligence the agents were supposed to be collecting was a priority for this investigation. After the conversation with each of our supervisors, not one corrective action was taken. A couple of days later, Chuck came back and told us that they discontinued night surveillance.

Just How Undercover Were We?

Another thing Frank and I were trying to get done was to have a dial number recorder or DNR, put on all phone lines going into the compound. A DNR captures numbers, but not voice. Frank was working with the acting supervisor, Earl, who kept telling us he had a friend who worked for the phone company and he could identify all the phone numbers in the compound. So we gave him a chance to let his friend produce the phone information we needed for the affidavit.

Frank was getting nowhere. After a week I asked him if he wanted me to try. He said, "Sure," so I called Earl and asked him the reason for the delay on the DNR.

"My friend is working on it, DiBetta," Earl said to me.

"But Earl, we don't need your friend. It would take me about 20 minutes to change the affidavit that was used for the photography, and turn it into a request for DNR," I said. "You just have to add one line to the court order requesting that the phone company identify all lines going into the compound."

"I'll get on my buddy," he replied and hung up.

Frustrated, Frank and I shared our experience with our supervisors. Chuck said he would look into it. You can imagined how ticked off we were in mid-January when Frank and I discovered that Earl did an undercover operation without telling us. We did not find out about this operation until a week or so after it was completed.

I'm assuming Chuck and Earl thought of this operation in an effort to get the phone numbers for the compound, instead of simply modifying the existing affidavit. To this day I still do not know how they picked the undercover agent for this deal. The agent was fairly new and had little or no experience doing undercover operations. He also had little, if any, technical knowledge about phone systems, or what we needed to know to obtain the phone numbers.

From what I learned, they set the deal up with the agent, Rick, posing as a UPS trainee. The plan was to have him ride with the UPS driver and try to get into the Davidian compound to look at their phone system. On the day of the operation, the first stop was at an FFL (federal firearms licensee), a gun shop called the Mag Bag, owned by the Davidians. This is where they got their firearms. They would funnel the firearms and do the paperwork through this gun shop and all the firearms and ammo would end up in the compound.

Agent Rick went to the gun shop posing as a UPS trainee and asked to use the bathroom. The man at the shop told him that the bathroom was not working and he should use the one at the Davidians' church. After the UPS driver and Agent Rick completed the deliveries at the gun shop, they headed up toward the compound.

When they arrived at the compound the number two man at the church, Schroeder, walked up to the delivery truck with a bucket and handed it to the undercover agent and said, "I hear you have to use the bathroom."

Well, to the agent's credit at least he pinched one out for the team. While he was away using the bathroom, the Davidians questioned the UPS driver. "I thought you had a dress code? Why does he have a ponytail?" Using some quick thinking, the driver replied, "It's his first day. He was told to get a haircut or he will lose his job." Having never gotten inside the compound, Agent Rick got back into the truck and they left.

Frank and I were upset by this operation for many reasons. Not only were we not told about it, but we could have briefed the undercover agent and come up with a better cover story. He could have carried a pager and told them his wife is pregnant. Then we could have paged him and had him ask to use the phone to call the hospital.

We also could've showed him how to use the A and I number. That's a number the phone company uses to identify a phone line. You pick up the phone, you dial a particular number and the phone number from which you're calling is repeated to you over the phone.

The whole thing was like amateur night, and what I'm sharing are not feelings benefitting from hindsight. This is what was going on during the Waco investigation.

Months after the compound burned, Under Secretary for Justice Brown came to talk to all the agents involved in the Waco investigation. Agent Rick believed he was being unfairly blamed for the loss of surprise when we served the warrant on Mount Carmel. He was later transferred to the L.A. office where he put his service revolver in his mouth and pulled the trigger right in front of another agent in the office. It was very sad.

I still do not understand why they did not even consult Frank and me on this operation. This action wasn't necessary, and we could have easily gotten this information by adding one line to the court order stating that the phone company had to identify all lines going into the compound.

In mid-February, a little more than a week before we executed the warrant on Mount Carmel, I called Earl again and asked him where the paperwork was for the DNR.

"DiBetta, I can't give birth," he said.

I wasn't really sure what the hell that was supposed to mean, but again I told him I would do the paperwork.

"I'll get to it," he replied and hung up.

Again, I told the supervisors. Collectively, they said it was pretty much the end of it because it was so close to serving warrants. I felt that we missed a great opportunity to find out how the Davidians were getting their parts for their reported automatic firearms. Tacitly, I felt we also missed a great opportunity to find out who was friendly or not, and if they had any local network in the compound area. The phone intelligence would have been a great help in those ways.

On February 1, Phil and Chuck had a meeting with the SRT team to discuss the upcoming activities in Waco. During this meeting, Chuck was looking for a name for this operation before they briefed headquarters. So we were all yelling out operational names and I yelled out, "Prairie Fire." To my surprise they liked the name and decided to go with it.

The next day Phil and Chuck left to go to headquarters in D.C., and while on the plane ASAC Chuck called me from the plane phone and told me they changed the operation name to Trojan Horse. Hanging up the phone, I shared the news with Frank.

"Why would he even bother telling me that?" I said in disbelief. "Can you imagine how much it cost to call me from the plane?" We both had a good laugh about that.

While we were able to laugh at the time, the truth is, the weeks leading up to the day on which we would serve the warrant were troubling. There were many unanswered questions, and I just couldn't put all the pieces together.

If the U/C house was so important, then why wasn't it run properly to gather the information they needed and claimed to be so important? If the U/C house was unimportant, then why would you risk the operation being exposed by having so many people in an U/C house?

Why weren't the type of cars and the protocol for arriving and departing the undercover house never properly addressed? The Texas Rangers told us some Davidians from the compound were trying to run the government undercover tags on the cars used in the operation.

Then there was the keg party held at the U/C house. They came up with this ruse in an effort to help convince the Davidians there were actually college students living there. They invited female agents to the house and the idea was to invite the Davidians to come over, get to know some of them and begin earning their trust in an effort to advance the investigation.

This wasn't a well-conceived idea. While some Davidians did come to the party, they were forbidden to drink by Koresh, so the idea of a beer party really wasn't that appealing to them. Maybe the agents would have fared better just having a cookout that wasn't as focused on alcohol.

At the time Frank and I didn't know if we were the problem and no one understood what we were trying to do. Maybe it was a management issue and a situation in which they thought they knew better than we did? This is something I'll never know.

Unfortunately, the direction for this case was set and soon the problems we'd already faced would seem like a walk in the park compared to what we were to come up against.

Chapter 5

THE WARRANT

A Bit of Background

A little background is in order before we get started on the stories related to serving the warrant on the Branch Davidians.

Even though the tactical command of this operation was in the hands of ATF leaders in the Houston office, the long arm of the D.C. headquarters would play an important role at Waco. In November or December, just months before we were to serve the warrant, our D.C. headquarters decided the AR-15s ATF carried had too much penetration power. The AR-15 is a semi automatic version of the M-16, and uses .223mm rounds. They gave these weapons to another agency—the IRS. I'm sure the warrants we did were 100 times more dangerous on an almost daily basis than those guys.

The reasoning behind the switch was a fear among ATF's leadership that with the high volume of urban warrants we were doing, if an agent fired the weapon it would go through a wall and hit someone on the other side. That was the whole point of the weapon! You wanted to shoot through walls under certain situations and have a weapon with strong knockdown power at a greater standoff distance.

Our headquarters instead opted for the H&K MP 5—a 9 mm, semi-automatic rifle. Yes, this was a well-made, great shooting, short assault rifle, but it did not generate the same muzzle velocity as the AR-15 and therefore did not have the penetration to go through many walls—especially reinforced walls like those built at the Mount Carmel compound in Waco.

Those same headquarters personnel also decided to limit the MP5s to a two-round burst, as opposed to a three-round burst, which is the standard used by the U.S. armed forces and just about every other law enforcement agency in the world. The story goes that the individual who did the ATF test shooting was not able to hold down the third shot in the burst, so ATF paid all kinds of money to have the firearm reengineered to only fire two-round bursts.

To this date you can't get anyone to admit they made this decision. On top of that, only members of the SRT were allowed to carry the two-burst machine guns. It bears saying again—many local law enforcement officers were already carrying the MP 5 as it was originally configured—to fire as a fully automatic, with a three-round burst, or as a single shot!

Our SRT was only allowed to have a few two-burst MP 5s on our team, while the rest of us had to carry MP 5s that only fired single shots. This was a sore spot with the team leaders of the three SRTs gathered to discuss the plans for serving the warrant.

Our team leaders understood the walls at the Davidians' compound were reinforced. So ASAC Chuck talked to the powers-that-be at headquarters, and they agreed in a memo to send us six AR-15 rifles. Ultimately, ATF headquarters ended up sending eight of them for this operation.

Another item newly issued to our SRT teams was a flash bang. A flash bang is a diversionary device, or stun grenade, that is designed to create a loud noise and a bright light to override a suspect's senses—stunning them for a few moments. The diversion allows the SRT to make a safer entry.

The device is maybe four inches tall, cylindrical and it has a protective shield with holes in it because the device gets very hot. It features a typical spoon ignition system like the one found on a regular hand grenade.

But as was the case with the AR-15s, ATF headquarters was afraid of these devices. SRTs were first trained in their use in September 1992. The original policy only permitted an SRT team to have one grenadier carrying three flash bangs. No one else was allowed to carry any of them. Nowadays, it seems, the SRT throws two or three every time before they walk into a room.

Prior to serving the warrant on the Branch Davidians and even during training for this entry, members of the SRT would talk about how the grenadier was never in the right place at the right time, no matter how well planned the operation. I guess it was old Murphy's Law again.

In addition to the flash bangs, there was also talk of having smoke grenades in case things went really bad at Mount Carmel. I don't know why, but that idea went nowhere.

By January 1993, I had more than 300 hard entries under my belt. The SRT teams were successful and we were fortunate in that our tactics always worked and we didn't get into any shootouts. This was impressive to me considering how many warrants we served in the high-crime areas around Houston as well as the other cities in our division. With that success, I think, the teams may have had a sense of complacency. We prepared under the false assumption that our past success would allow us to carry out this plan without incident.

Final Training

On February 25, 1993, the SRT teams from Dallas, Houston and New Orleans headed to Fort Hood for practice training only days before March 1—the day we were scheduled to serve the warrant at Mount Carmel. Fort Hood had a huge mount site: a fake city the military uses to train for urban fighting. It also featured an underground tunnel system for training, which my team ended up using because of our specific role on the day of the warrant. Frank and I had dual roles. We were on the Houston SRT and also continued to serve as Tactical Operations Officers (TOO).

Keep in mind that at this time, ATF was a relatively small agency and had a limited budget, even for an operation such as this one. We were the only technical guys. Once at Fort Hood, Frank and I were often required to check on recoding radios for the vehicles and driving to the Waco command post to set up phones and faxes. While working in the TOO role, we missed the main briefing before the operation. We didn't worry too much about that, since typically before any mission there was a final briefing, just before serving the warrant, when we would receive last minute information and any change of plans.

Training without factual intelligence left the SRT estimating how many rooms were on the first floor by the window count. As we practiced making entry and clearing that same number of rooms, we realized it took too long. The timing of this phase of the operation was critical for two reasons. First, without detailed knowledge of what we'd encounter once inside the building, the element of surprise was paramount. Second, we needed to be quick in order to keep the Davidians from mounting a counter attack.

In an effort to improve time, we tried adding my team to the end of the main entry team to see if that would speed things up. It was such

The Compound

The Davidian compound consisted of a main building, which had many small rooms along its front used for day-to-day living. To the left of the main building there appeared to be a bunker being built just below the ground. We were told there was a tunnel that connected the bunker to a location under the front part of the main building. We weren't certain of exactly where it led.

The photo is of the compound on March 1 the day after we served the warrant. There is a large amount of debris surrounding the compound from where the houses were torn down. Also visible are all the ATVs and go-carts the Davidians allegedly obtained through the use of credit card and check fraud schemes. From the picture the two trailers used when we tried to serve the warrant remain in place. Look how small they look compared to the size of the compound.

To the left of the building was what appeared to be a tall water tower. In reality, it was a sniper's position. The tower was constructed with wooden floors and five landings. Inside, a metal ladder was used extending from the ground to the top of the structure. It was built with kick plates on each level so a gunman could quickly kick it open and establish a shooting position. Towards the back of the compound was what looked like a big pool; this is where the Davidians were collecting water for use at the compound.

All the way to the right of the building and going from the front to the back in the shape of an "L" was the main auditorium. This is where Koresh's band practiced. This is the same location where Koresh gave his sermons, some of which lasted for 12 hours at a time. He would preach for so long that he would urinate in a bucket in front of everybody and use bathroom breaks as a method of control over his congregation.

On the second floor of this wing was the armory. This was the location of the well-recognized window shootout between the Davidians and the ATF agents on the roof. This was the scene shown on most news stations.

In the center of the main building was a tower. Koresh used the tower as his private living quarters. It was the only place in the building that was air-conditioned. The tower was the only place where there was any alcohol and Koresh was the only person permitted to have it. His preference was beer.

a large complex it really didn't matter. Even though our team leader knew the plan was flawed—he knew we couldn't clear that much ground in the allotted time—it was decided by the leaders to stick with the plan as it was designed. Now the element of surprise would be even more imperative to the success of this operation. At the time, I felt a little unsettled, but I had overall confidence in the planning, especially our objectives in getting on the roof and then accessing the armory where the compound's weapons were stored. Without their weapons, or their main weapons, I thought we had a good shot. I believe that was the overall consensus among the agents. Due to all the work and focus on preparing for the warrant, there wasn't much time for an agent in my role to spend reevaluating the plan. I believed this was going to be an early morning warrant, as was the case most of the time.

Operation Trojan Horse

The original plan for Operation Trojan Horse was to use two pickup trucks each pulling a gooseneck cattle trailer. Each trailer would carry roughly 40 agents. The trailers were made to look like cattle transports commonly used in the area. The trailers had thin plywood added to the sides with plastic and canvas draped over the top and then secured to the plywood siding. Other than complaining about how thin the plywood was, our teams thought the trailers were a good idea for getting us close to the isolated compound. After the fire destroyed the compound, some of the Davidians were interviewed and admitted the cattle trailers confused them. They thought we were lost and looking for directions. Still, they were a long way from being armored vehicles!

My team consisted of six agents, with me in the lead. I carried a ballistic bunker, which was about two feet wide, three feet long with a light centered on the top. A battery pack and ballistic window were embedded in the bunker. It weighed about 30 pounds. We were supposed to be assisted by two more agents who sat in the cab of the pickup truck pulling our trailer. Their job was to take custody of any Davidians we might encounter.

I later heard that during the briefings—the ones missed because of TOO duties—our team leaders shared that they expected 30 Davidians to be working on the underground bunker system when we arrived at the compound. It was believed the Davidians would be all men and digging with picks and shovels. If I had known this, I would have raised an objection to the Agent-Davidian ratio. We would have been outmanned. Even if we were able to control the situation, we weren't carrying enough flex cuffs to properly contain the men if we were able to subdue them.

I was to be the first agent off the first trailer. Our team was to dismount, head toward the compound's underground bunker and enter an underground tunnel system through a 4-foot doorway. Then the team was to pass through a buried bus the Davidians used as a shooting range for their automatic weapons. Next, we'd make way through more tunneling that led to the trap door leading into the main building. Once there, we were to make contact with the other teams and assist them with clearing the inside of the building.

Our knowledge of the main building's design was based on information from several sources. In particular, Davidians who once lived on the compound who were interviewed, aerial photos, as well as information from public records. Unfortunately, there wasn't much useful information coming out of the U/C house.

We practiced and practiced and practiced, for two long days. Our plan required the element of surprise and we simulated our dismount from the vehicles as though we had arrived at the compound completely undetected. The operation was to be aborted if there was a report of shots being fired before we dismounted. But the leaders wanted us to also practice simulating dismounts as if shots were fired and the vehicles had to stop short of the compound.

The first time they stopped the trailers, they told us we were taking fire from the compound and asked us what we should do? Being assigned as the first one off the first trailer, I got off, and not knowing where the simulated compound was, I went in the wrong direction. I was immediately corrected.

When we went back to the trailer, one of the agents said, "This is just like the Monty Python movie, *Monty Python and the Holy Grail*. When they were attacked by a killer rabbit, and forced to retreat, they all yell 'run away, run away!'"

A few other agents overheard this and the next time we did the exercise, several agents exiting the trailer started yelling, "Run away. Run away." It was funnier when it happened. The thing was, this was our only contingency plan—get off the trailers and run away from the compound.

Easier in planning but the compound was on high, wide-open ground with some distance to reach cover of any kind in any direction. Maybe it's not surprising then that 20 years later one of the team leaders claimed there was no contingency plan. I guess he just forgot his?

During this training, it became more and more clear to me just how big the compound really was because of the large mockups we were training on, and the amount of time it took us to clear them. At this time I began to notice how our leaders seemed to be increasingly influenced by the military advisors that were working with us.

Some of these military advisors suggested we all test fire our weapons before going out on this mission just like the military does before each of its operations. At the end of our second and last day of training, we all got our pistols and MP 5s out, and shot at a log on the mount site. This was something we never did. We had great trust in our weapons, and thought this was a strange ritual. Just like in sports, you don't want to stray from your regular routine before a big game. To me, our leadership started thinking more like the military and less like a law enforcement group. My experience is in both the military and law enforcement. In the military you have air support and armored vehicles.

Throughout the training at Fort Hood, they had us all sleeping in open barracks with bunk beds. Remember Don, the guy who was put in charge of the U/C house? He was also the driver of the first trailer. On the night before we went into action, he was sleeping about 10 bunks from where I was tossing and turning because he snored so loud it actually hurt my ears. I couldn't take it anymore, so I got up to find him, which was easy due to the sound, then demanded he roll over to stop the snoring.

SAC Phil and ASAC Chuck decided to change the date of the warrant from Monday, March 1 to Sunday, February 28. Our team leaders notified us late on the 26th. The change was made because a local paper was to publish an article about the Davidians on the 28th.

Our leaders believed that if the article came out, then other articles would follow, possibly putting the Davidians on a higher state of alert. This would affect the element of surprise, and we'd been drilled that the element of surprise was imperative, a key factor in this plan, and essential to the success of this operation.

As a precaution, a few days before the operation, our leadership had called the local ambulance company. They called to request several ambulances be on standby in case of injury during the serving of the warrant. Unbeknownst to our leaders, the ambulance dispatcher was dating a cameraman for a local TV news station. Of course, the dispatcher told her boyfriend, so in the early morning hours of February 28, a TV crew was driving around on the roads near the compound looking for our staging area.

It's Go Time

We awoke at 3:30 a.m. on the morning of the 28th to get dressed, get our gear together and hit the road. We were instructed to drive our own cars, which nearly all of us did. We left Fort Hood about 6:30 a.m. The caravan stretched for nearly a mile. After about an hour, we arrived at our Waco meeting spot—an old arena with a large parking lot. Our leadership kept emphasizing operational security, but the first thing I saw was an agent, wearing his ATF jacket, directing traffic in the middle of the road. This was the beginning of a long day!

So far, we'd alerted the media via a request for an ambulance, built a mile-long caravan of vehicles driving from Fort Hood to Waco, and had an essentially uniformed agent in the middle of the street directing traffic. Surprise was imperative!

While we were traveling to Waco from Fort Hood, the SRT snipers had gone to the U/C house to take up positions around the compound. The original plan was to put a sniper on each of the four sides of the compound. For some reason they decided not to cover one side of the compound, they manned three positions with four snipers.

The snipers traveled in a van and parked the van at the U/C house. They locked the van and set the alarm. Why? I have no idea. Back then, car alarms weren't as shielded as they are now. For instance, if I would take my government car and drive through a parking lot and then key, or turn on my radio to transmit, it would set off everyone's car alarm.

You know what's coming, don't you? An agent in the U/C house keyed his microphone to transmit a radio message and he set off the van's alarm. I don't know if you've ever been out in the country early in the morning, but sound travels really well. I can't say if this is another of the factors compromising the element of surprise, but it was just one more thing that happened that day.

The van's alarm went off and the lights flashed for several minutes in an area accustomed to dead silence. The agents inside the U/C house did not have the keys, so they broke the hood of the van and ripped out the alarm's speaker.

Back at our staging area, someone had the brilliant idea to write our blood type on our neck with a ballpoint pen. I thought this was ridiculous and told another agent.

"I don't care if you had a note from God, there is not a hospital in this country that won't type check you before they do any blood transfusion," I said to him. This was another idea the team leaders got from the military. The agent agreed, but we took our place at the end of the line anyway. The pen they used was a cheap ballpoint and not a Sharpie™ or other type of permanent marker. Needless to say it was not writing very well, so they would press the pen into your neck until you could either see the ink or enough skin was scraped and your blood type showed up as a scratch! I went into the bathroom and put some cold water on my neck where my blood type was carved into my skin! That just ticked me off.

An Ominous Start

Gathered in the arena, the team became restless as warrants were almost always served at 6 a.m. on the nose. This usually gave us the element of surprise to catch the subjects either sleeping or just getting up. We had been waiting and waiting and waiting.

I, and many of my fellow agents, thought it was odd that we still hadn't had our final briefing. Then, around 9 a.m. ASAC Chuck ran in and yelled, "Hurry!! Everybody suit up. They know we're coming. They know ATF and the National Guard are coming."

I thought it weird that he mentioned the National Guard, because we did not have any National Guard assets with us other than some helicopters that SAC Phil was using as an observation/command center. We had been told time and again that the element of surprise was so important, and by Chuck's own words, we'd already lost it. In addition, the commander in the U/C house never alerted the command center that there were no signs of men working in the bunker. It's another indication that the element of surprise had been compromised. But the operation was still on.

Every one jumped up and started to get ready. I could sense everyone was anxious and ready to get this operation under way. We all began to suit up, and all wore the same basic gear—BDUs, black Army surplus boots, knee and elbow pads, military style Kevlar helmet, and fire resistant black Nomex gloves. I wore glasses.

I put on my web gear, a utility belt held up by a pair of suspenders that was designed to carry my holstered 9mm Sig Sauer, extra pistol ammo (two clips), a canteen of water, a bayonet for searching and probing, hand cuffs and a Leatherman tool. Next was my level 3 ballistic vest, which held a ballistic breastplate capable of stopping a .30-06 round. On top of that I wore a load-bearing vest in which I carried a five-shot revolver with extra rounds and extra ammunition for all the firearms used by agents involved in the operation—the MP 5, AR-15, a 12-gauge Remington 870 shotgun. I also stuck in some parachute cord, a door stop and blood stoppers. On my back I had a radio that attached to an ear piece, flex cuffs, a four D-cell MAG-LITE flashlight and another pair of handcuffs. Just to be certain, I also carried a .38 Model 66 Smith and Weston revolver as backup, and a king-sized Snickers for later.

In total it was 60 pounds of gear, including the bunker. I never really felt the weight; I must have had so much adrenaline coursing through my veins. We left the briefing center to load up on the cattle trailers. In the parking lot I ran into Steve Willis. He had a shotgun in his hand and I remember telling him, "This is pretty exciting. Just be careful today." As I grabbed the top of his vest and shook him, we both laughed. That was last time I saw him alive.

While we were waiting at the arena, events were unfolding elsewhere. It was later learned and verified through post-investigation interviews that about this time, the news crew looking for us out on the road encountered one of the Davidians who worked for the Postal Service. Since it was a rural route, the guy drove a private car with U.S. Mail lettered on a rack with two yellow lights on top of the vehicle.

The news crew told the postal employee, "You better get out of here. ATF and the National Guard are coming." The Davidian just drove off. To this day I don't know why the postal employee was out on a Sunday, but I'm sure he high-tailed it back to the compound using back roads and warned Koresh we were coming.

Because ASAC Chuck moved up the warrant date, and since he had such poor intelligence from the U/C house on exactly what was going on at the compound that Sunday, he decided to ask the undercover agent with the most contact with Koresh, to go to the compound to see what was going on.

The agent's name was Robert. This next part of my story is based on information I received directly from him as well as from the sniper assigned to cover the front of the compound from the U/C house. I can only imagine the fear this agent felt going into a compound, knowing we were about to execute the warrant.

As he walked up to the front door of the main building, Robert was met by Koresh and brought inside via the front entrance. Koresh always limited where Robert could go inside the house, and on this visit Koresh made it clear through his nonverbal actions that Robert was allowed to go no further than the small area inside the front door.

Koresh asked Robert to pray with him, which he did. He then said, "Good luck today, Robert," as he walked the agent to the door and said good-bye.

Robert believed very strongly that Koresh knew something was going to happen that day. As he walked back to the U/C house, an agent inside the house opened the window where a camera with a very big lens was located. It was set up in such a way that the camera was clearly visible to Robert as he walked down the road from the compound.

Upon entering the U/C house Robert yelled, "I could see the camera from the driveway of the compound," and immediately threw a towel over it. The agent who set up this equipment was the same one whom had weeks earlier asked me how to use a tripod.

Robert immediately got on the phone with ASAC Chuck and told him, "The Davidians know we are coming." The sniper overheard the conversation and began packing up his sniper rifle and other equipment. He believed the execution of the warrant would be called off.

It's my belief that shortly after this phone call, ASAC Chuck came into the briefing area and told us to mount up for the operation. This was the first time in my career we did not have a final briefing before we went to execute a warrant.

It is Show Time

We were finally on our way. By now we all knew our positions in the trailer, and it went quickly. Being the first one off the first trailer, I had the unique vantage point looking out the back of the trailer and seeing the second truck and trailer behind us. Since I carried a bunker, I grabbed the overhead supports of the trailer while holding the bunker in my other hand. We were all very quiet.

We were about 15 minutes away from the compound and moving along at a pretty good clip on the EE Ranch Road, which would carry us all the way to the front of the compound. Our driver, Don, was traveling much too fast when he took a rather sharp turn. If I didn't have hold of the roof support, I would've fallen over.

I can vividly recall the expressions of horror on the faces of the guys in the truck behind us after we made this turn. Their eyes were huge and they started yelling at each other. In the midst of the excitement of this near miss, over the radio we heard the "go" word, "Showtime." The mission was on.

I sometimes think back on how many things would've changed if he had tipped the trailer and the warrant was never executed.

Shots Fired

Minutes before our arrival at the compound, the two helicopters used by SAC Phil as an aerial command post, were flying over the compound. The Davidians, who were already setting an ambush for us, began shooting at them. I recall they shot both of the helicopters. A bullet tore through an agent's BTU jacket, but luckily it did not injure him.

The National Guard's helicopter policy was that if they ever took fire they would immediately land the helicopter and assess the damage. And that's what they did. They landed in a field maybe a half-mile from the compound.

As we were turning up the horseshoe driveway to the compound, I heard over the radio, "Shots fired. Shots fired." I reached for my pistol. Since shots were fired, I expected the trailers to stop, and we would dismount, run away or surround the compound and wait for further instruction depending on how far up the drive we'd gone. The trailers never stopped. We continued to drive right up to the front of the compound. Once the trailer stopped, the agent behind me unhooked the locking mechanism on the gate. I pushed the gate open with my ballistic shield and stepped off.

What do they say in the Army? Something like, as soon as the first soldier puts boots on the ground, you throw out your plan. I took one step and immediately began to hear gunfire in front and to the right of me.

If you asked me how many steps I took from the trailer to the bunker's entrance, a hole in the ground at the opening of the tunnel—I would've told you five. The actual distance was just less than 50 yards.

As I ran, the volume of gunfire got louder, and I remember seeing bullets kicking up the dirt in rapid fire, as if from a machine gun. I had an earpiece in one ear and an earplug in the other anticipating the possible use of flash bang in the tunnel. But I do know the distinct sound of gunfire. Just as in the military, a big part of training is completing the mission. I believed my best bet for survival was to get into that hole given the rate of fire we were taking.

I also remember quickly turning around to see who was behind me and seeing explosions. At the time, I thought it was our grenadiers throwing flash bangs, but it was actually the Davidians. They had made actual hand grenades from the simulated grenades they bought on the open market. Later I discovered they welded a piece of metal to cover the hole on the bottom and fashioned some type of fusing. Voila! You have a homemade grenade. Today it's a design easily found on the Internet.

The problem with the Davidians' grenades was that they added a chemical to the black powder. The Davidians thought it would add to the explosive power of their grenades, but it only caused the black powder to get wet. Black powder doesn't like to be wet and as a result, we were fortunate. Most of the agents who were hit with the grenades just received superficial wounds—ripped BDUs and minimal penetration to the skin.

After my sprint across the front of the compound to my little no man's land, I jumped into the hole and covered myself with the ballistic shield I was carrying. Even with the additional 60 pounds, when I jumped into that hole I felt like it weighed nothing at all. Believe it or not, my first reaction was to start laughing. I remember thinking, *This is ridiculous. The volume of gunfire sounded like the opening scene of the Normandy landing in the movie "Saving Private Ryan."* That's how much volume of fire was in our direction. I also remembered, *I am waiting to hear the screams.*

I was worried the Davidians would start shooting at the trailers, as it took us 10 or 15 seconds to empty the trailers during training. Fortunately for us, they did not even attempt to shoot at the trailers as we were dismounting.

Having settled into the hole, I used my shield to cover my left side as I was taking a lot of fire near my left shoulder and directly over my head. But every now and then a bullet would hit so close I would try to press myself tighter into the dirt.

Strange things go through your mind in a situation like this. *I am a nice guy. Why would anybody be shooting at me?*

I quickly looked where we were supposed enter the tunnel. It was not a four-foot entrance as we were told. It was maybe one foot high and about 3 1/2 feet wide.

The only way in or out of that underground passage was either headfirst or feet first. With all of gunfire going on, it would have been an impossible entry. As I studied the entrance, I suddenly saw a right booted foot, and then a left.

"Police! Come out! Police! Come out mother f'er! Come out or I'll kill you! Police! Come out," I yelled as loudly as I could. And just as suddenly as they appeared, the boots disappeared.

Now, I could have shot him, but there was so much confusion and he was wearing the same type of Army boots that I was wearing. I could not see the color of his pants, and figured there was a real possibility it could've have been one of our guys. All I can say is it would have hurt like hell if I had shot him in the ankle.

Being on the defensive, I took out three light sticks, un-wrapped them, snapped the chemicals inside that lit them up then threw them into the bunker's entrance. It didn't really help, as all I could see was the light sticks and nothing else. I figured if anybody broke the plane of those light sticks, I would shoot them right then and there. The gunfire then seemed to decrease a little in my direction.

The Davidians had a sniper positioned up in the water tower. I am guessing he was the one who was shooting so close to my left side. I figured the gunman concentrated on me a bit, because I was the first one off the trailer. Fortunately, one of our agents upon exiting the first trailer saw the man on the water tower. Using only the front sight of his MP5, he fired a single round, eliminating the sniper. What an amazing round.

Getting my wits about me, I realized I was supposed to have five other team members with me in the hole, yet I was by myself. With this volume of gunfire, was I the only survivor?

I quickly surveyed the surrounding area outside the hole and saw my bunker mate, or wingman, maybe 15 feet directly in front of me. He was standing up and unprotected. Walt was left-handed and shooting with his pistol extended straight out, unsupported. While he was returning fire the bullets were spraying up dirt all around his feet.

I screamed, "Walt! Get your butt down! Get your butt down!"

He looked at me, looked back at his target, fired a couple more shots, squatted down and he ran over to the hole where I was. "Dave, I am mad," Walt exclaimed upon landing next to me.

"Reload your gun," I replied to him.

"Dave, I am really mad!" I did not look at his face as I was still looking around.

"Walt, reload your gun."

"Dave, I'm really mad."

"Walt, reload your f'ing gun!" At that point he did reload. In the midst of the gunfire, all I kept thinking was: *These jerks. When they charge us, at least our guns will be fully loaded.*

Turning to Walt, I said, "There's someone on the other side of that opening. I threw three light sticks in there, but we need to cover the entrance."

"Do you have a knife with you?" I asked him.

"Yeah."

"Dig up some dirt and use it to cover the hole. At least that way the person inside won't hear or see our movements, and if he does try to shoot us we will see the dirt being disturbed," I said. "While you are filling up the hole, keep an eye on the opening, and I'll keep a lookout all around us."

At this point, Walt was behind me digging away at the dirt. Out of the corner of my eye I see little chunks of dirt being thrown toward the entrance. I snapped around.

"Let me see your knife," I yelled.

He held up one of those Swiss Army knives that was maybe three-inches long and carried a toothpick!

"You're f'ing killing me," I said as I pulled out my bayonet and handed it to him.

With the right tool, he quickly filled the entrance to the bunker. You could not dig with your hands, especially with the light mist falling that morning. Our hole had been dug in what the farmers called black clay. The earth was very dense and it had turned dark from the mist. With the entrance to the bunker blocked, I felt more comfortable moving around.

I did not know where my team was. There was no real radio chatter. Everybody was just hunkered down because of the intense fire being thrown at us by the Davidians. With constant gunfire that seemed to be everywhere at once, and occasional explosions, I decided to find any other members of my team. The talk in the news reports about this day claimed the gun battle lasted 45 minutes. In reality, we were taking fire from the time we arrived until the time we left, which was around noon. By my math that's 2 1/2 hours.

Staying to the right side of the bunker's entrance, I elevated myself a bit more to see what was going on. Twenty or twenty-five yards to the right of me was an agent who'd been shot. He was pale as paper and his shirt was saturated and very dark. I could tell he was in bad shape.

"Do you have any first aid," I hollered at him. I don't know if he responded or not, or if he had even heard me. I'm not certain, but I believe not everyone had a radio that day. "Put mud on it. Put mud on it," I yelled. That would stop the bleeding since there was no other alternative.

Walt suggested we should try to throw him some first aid. I told him it was too far and more than likely it would fall into a place that wouldn't do any good.

Just then the radio chatter began to pick up. Our team leader was trying to determine where everybody was. I heard my team leader ask, "DiBetta where are you?" I was relieved to know that someone was going to know where we were.

"I'm in the hole," I said.

"DiBetta where are you?" he repeated.

"I'm in the bunker entrance hole," I replied with a bit more emphasis.

Then came the reply that chilled me. "DiBetta, we don't know where you are," came the reply.

"I'm in the f'ing hole! I'm in the f'ing hole!"

"Okay."

It just goes to show you when you use good police verbiage, it makes a message so much clearer!

ATF had an Air Wing, and at one time it was useful. But there'd been a big scandal when the supervisor for the Air Wing was arrested for stealing more than $2 million from ATF. This supervisor/pilot opened a fueling business at a local airport. He had the ATF planes fly there to refuel and, from what I'd heard, he would shortchange them as well as submit bogus invoices for payment.

Anyway, after the scandal ATF got five or six, surplus, Vietnam era, OV-10s. This plane was used as a spotter plane in Vietnam. The military would fly low over the treetops to draw fire and then call in artillery to bombard the areas from which they were taking fire.

The plane was a two-seater, so you could only transport one person. It also had a high stall speed, so you couldn't fly slowly over a particular area for surveillance and it couldn't position itself on station to carry a repeater to transmit.

It had a flare system that used infrared, but it was one of the first generations and never worked. They were cost prohibitive to fix, and because it was a military plane, they were loud. The ATF also saw fit to paint them dark blue with a fire engine red stripe down the side. They really stood out in the sky.

Well, of course, we had our plane out for this operation and the pilot was doing circles over the compound. But its engine was so loud and so close to the ground that you had trouble hearing other people talking on the radio or even the person next to you asking a question.

I radioed to ask if the plane could determine the source of the fire that had us pinned down. "I'm right in front of the bunker, that's my 12 o'clock. Tell me from what point we're getting all this fire."

I did this twice without ever getting a response. Anytime any one of our guys moved, the Davidians would counter with bursts of automatic machine gun fire—and there was a lot of fire. Eventually, ATF got the plane to leave the area. I believe this is just one more example of how unprepared our leadership team was in regard to their judgment on field operations.

The roar of airplane's engine had just softened, when it was replaced by the distinct sound of a .50 caliber weapon being fired. I knew this because I was a .50 gunner in the Army.

"We need help over here. We need help now," said Walt, yelling into his radio.

"That's a .50 caliber gun being fired," I said to him over the din of the fire. "With all this dirt around us, we're actually in a pretty good place."

Shortly afterwards, I heard on the radio that my TOO partner, Frank, had been shot in the leg. Immediately after that someone else said, "Steve (Willis) is down." I do not know what I was thinking, but I got on the radio and told Frank I would be right over. I asked him for his location. Then my radio blared with warnings from multiple agents to stay where I was. Pretty sound advice, so I did.

Pinned Down

All this occurred in just 30 minutes, although to be honest, I really had no sense of time. If you had asked me how long we were there I would have guessed an hour or so.

When there was a lull in the gunfire, I wondered what our exit strategy would be. I knew police cars couldn't come up the road. It was possible an armored vehicle could try, but the plating on it would not stop the .50 caliber Barrett semiautomatic rifle. I was told later that it was fixed with what's called a "hellfire" switch, which enables the gun to fire like an automatic weapon when you pull the trigger.

The Davidians had a pretty good strategy. They used a three-person team on this weapon. One was the shooter, the second was the loader/spotter and the third acted as the tripod for the weapon. The tripod put the weapon on his shoulder. They positioned themselves away from the windows, so it was difficult for our snipers to see their muzzle flash. They fired three, three-round bursts then moved to another window to shoot.

Not having been provided with an actionable plan, I began thinking of stripping off what equipment I didn't need and low-crawling it out of there under the cover of darkness. I remember hearing all kinds of sounds as the gun battle progressed. Bullets were coming in sounding like artillery pieces. They'd hit something and make a whirlwind sound flying overhead. It sounded as though shots were coming from all around us.

Walt and I were beginning to hear talk over the radio about a plan to get the wounded agent in front of us some first aid or rescue. Nobody had any good ideas—there was just too much gunfire. As if things weren't interesting enough, Walt who was still by my side, turned to me and said, "I have to take a leak."

"Just go in your pants."

"No way!" he exclaimed back at me with a defiant voice.

"What? Are you gonna' do it now? We're in the middle of a gun fight!" To this day I do not know what happened—nor do I want to know. I never looked at him.

The bullets continued over our heads and I needed to determine the location of that gunman pinning us down. I hoped we could then blindly direct fire into that area and maybe push them back and prevent them from firing at us every time we moved.

I was getting nowhere on the radio, so I tried doing a series of quick peeks. This is where you pop up, take a look then zip back down. I felt like a character in that Whac-a-mole arcade game.

I'd pop up and just look in a particular area. As soon as I'd drop down, a round of machine gun fire would fly over my head. I would move over a little bit to my left, and I popped up again to look at a different section. Again, as soon as I was safely back in the hole, the rounds zipped over my head.

I had moved over to my right, and for a third time I shot up and looked in an area I had not checked out before. For a third time I made it back into the hole before the rounds zipped over my head. Unfortunately, I never located the shooters.

After this, Walt said to me, "Dave, I have got to tell you something I haven't told anyone else."

I'm thinking to myself, "Holy crap. What now?" He then shared with me that his wife was pregnant and I was the first one to know.

"Well, I have to tell you something too," I said to him.

"What?"

"Before I left, our income tax forms were done and I didn't sign them." Don't ask me why I said that, but it was the first thing that popped into my head.

After about an hour, there was a lull in radio traffic. I got on the radio and said, "Sight, sight, watch sight." We'd recently been told that under stressful situations you might begin to ignore your gun sights. If you're not taking the time to properly aim your weapon, then your target picture is off and you are essentially wasting ammunition. In our situation, we had no resupply options and we certainly had no idea how long we'd be there. I don't know if my reminders did any good or not.

By now I knew we were in it for the long haul, and had to make every round count. There was no back up coming any time soon.

I don't know how long we were in that hole, but it seemed like forever. Finally, word came over the radio about an effort to make contact with the compound. Remember, because we didn't do a thing with the Davidians' phone system, we didn't have their telephone number!

Fortunately, the Davidians living next-door to the U/C house were taken into custody and told us the compound's telephone number was on their refrigerator. One of our agents went over, got the phone number and initiated communications with the Davidians. During this time, all kinds of phone calls were going on out there—including the ones we made to the Davidians, the 911 call the Davidians made to the Sheriff's office, and our command center calling everyone!

Cease-Fire

ATF finally got through to the Davidians, and Koresh agreed to a cease-fire. After hearing that, I turned to Walt and told him to stay down for a second while I took another peek. I popped up again and when I dropped back down, another burst of machine gun fire ripped over my head. Yeah, right! Some cease-fire!

My original team was behind the bulldozer located about halfway between our trailer and the hole in which Walt and I were located. They started yelling, "Cease-fire! Cease-fire!"

"Get the hell out of here. You're trespassing," yelled one of the Davidians from a location at the side the compound from which heavy fire had been coming.

"We're trying," came the ATF reply from the agents behind the bulldozer. "We have to get a wounded agent in front of you and then we'll get out of here."

The Davidians agreed.

"Stay down," I said to Walt as I began to climb from the hole to retrieve the wounded agent with my gun still in hand.

As soon as I stood up, an agent from behind the bulldozer cut across in front of me to assist our downed man. Since I was up, I decided to cover the agent with my pistol, looking around to see any Davidians for later identification and to scope out the property for anything that might be useful to us in the coming days.

Just as he was bringing the wounded agent in front of me, ASAC Chuck yelled from the top of the hole. "Come on, DiBetta; let's get the hell out of here."

I yelled, "Chuck, I am covering down."

Once the agents with the wounded man were clear, I turned around. It was no more than four seconds after he yelled to me, and he was gone.

"That mother f'er!"

I went to the back of the hole and tried to get out. I first lifted the bunker out and then I tried to climb out, but the damn soupy clay was just too slippery. I pulled out my knife, stuck it into the ground and began pulling myself up. But I hadn't driven the blade deep enough and I fell back in the hole. People have often asked me if I was scared and I can honestly say no—at least not until that point. Still struggling to get out of the muddy hole, I began to worry I might get left behind. Looking around, I didn't see anyone.

Suddenly, from out of nowhere, Harry, one of the support agents, came up from behind and said, "Let me give you a hand."

I had my bayonet in my hand and he asked, "You're not leaving anything behind are you?"

"Hell no," I said.

The Long Walk

We decided not to walk in front of the compound, but to walk through the field and straight to the compound's entrance along the road.

In one of the videos taken that day, there's footage of agents carrying a wounded agent. Walking through the field are three figures—Harry, Walt and me.

We were maybe 20 feet from the hole at the site of one of the biggest gun battles in U.S. law enforcement history. That's when Walt turns to the compound, lifts up his left arm, gives them the finger, and yells at the top of his lungs, "Screw you, you mother f'er! We're going to come back and kick your butt."

Now, it wasn't that I disagreed with anything he said, but to say it with all the weapons they had in the compound and being in the middle of a field without the safety of our hole?

I lifted up my vest and sunk my head down into it.

"Shut the hell up!" I yelled at him. "If you don't shut up, I will shoot you myself."

Remember, we were walking through an open meadow, and their height superiority gave them a fantastic field of fire. I was just waiting for the sting from being shot, but fortunately we got to the road safely.

The road was part of the circular driveway that led to the EE Ranch Road. Agents were walking with their hands up as if in surrender. We were in total confusion. An ambulance arrived that was driven by two agents, because the ambulance crew refused to get too close to the action. As I walked by, it was being loaded with the wounded and the dead.

All the agents in the area started heading down the driveway. There was no leadership at all. I remember turning around and just looking to see if the Davidians were going to run out of the building and start shooting us.

If they had done that, they would have gotten a good bunch of us before anybody would have reacted. We were lucky that did not happen.

We got to the main road looking like a defeated army. I remember stopping where the driveway met the road and looked back to discover that no one was covering our withdrawal.

I stood there and then a TV cameraman stood next to me, while I was absorbing what just happened and contemplating what was coming next. A few other agents did turnaround, but that was it. Everybody just kept walking up the road to an intersection, where more ambulances were waiting.

As we were walking, vehicles passed us carrying the dead and wounded agents. I remember a pickup truck, its tailgate down and an agent wrapped in a blanket in the truck bed, was captured on film as it made its way to the waiting ambulances.

Another agent, whom I worked with closely when I first arrived to Texas, was walking up the road. He showed me his hand. His thumb was shot off. He said his job was to open the front door of the main building. The door had two panels to it, but the Davidians only used the left side as you faced the door from the outside.

He told me he saw Koresh at the door and yelled for him to get down. Koresh just smiled at him and went inside the compound, closing the door behind him. Standing in front of the right door panel, this agent reached to grab the doorknob. He said it literally exploded from gunfire, and the top of his thumb was shot off.

It wasn't bleeding too badly. I told him to keep it raised above his heart, and he was keeping pressure on it. As soon as he arrived at the intersection, he boarded an ambulance and went to the hospital.

It's amazing how patterns developed. Had the Davidians used both sides of the door, this agent surely would've been shot to death. The Davidians only thought to shoot at the side of the door they used, thus saving the agent's life.

The ambulances were pretty full. Four agents were killed and 16 wounded. We considered ourselves lucky with those numbers. The Texas Ranger's report estimated the Davidians fired between 12-15,000 rounds on that day. The report stated we returned 1,100-1,500 rounds.

Later on, we learned from the Davidians, they believed their weapons could not penetrate our body armor. That's why most of the wounded had lower torso and leg shots. Of the four agents killed, three were hit with headshots and one received a gunshot just below the neck and above the vest.

Back at the intersection, I saw Steve's body still lying in the road. I guess the ambulances were being used for the wounded first. When I first saw Steve on the road, a cameraman, who walked down the road with me, began to videotape his body in the street.

A female agent who was telling the cameraman to, "Get the hell out here and turn off the camera" drew my attention to this scene.

At first he didn't respond to her, so I began walking toward him. He then backed off. I remember she continued yelling at him. She had things well in hand.

I turned toward Steve, and fortunately, while they were carrying him his vest covered his head. He had been shot in the head. I looked over his body and for some reason was struck by the fact that his wristwatch just keep ticking. I said a quiet prayer and left. As his supervisor, Curtis, came over and stayed by Steve's side until he was taken away.

At his funeral, I told his sister that he returned a lot of fire with his shotgun. Later, I discovered he had been told to put the shotgun away. All he had was his 9 mm pistol. I felt terrible that I had given her bad information. After this was all over, one of the jobs as TOO was the responsibility to manage our team's equipment. When Steve's pistol came back to us, it had to two empty clips and a clip only half full. You knew he gave a good account of himself that day.

Just then a Texas State Trooper pulled up. He said he had a Davidian in custody who'd been trying to get back into the compound.

"Your people are a bunch of cowards," I said as I bent into the car. Then I peppered him with a few other police adjectives.

The trooper also had a cell phone with him. Back then cell phone minutes were very expensive, but he was kind enough to let me call home.

ATF originally planned to serve the warrant on Monday, March 1, but as I explained earlier, they decided to change it to Sunday. I didn't tell my wife, Judy.

I figured we would do the warrant; I'd call her later in the day and tell her it was over. I just didn't want her to worry. Judy was out washing the car when she received a phone call from friends in Delaware asking her if I was all right. They told her the news was reporting ATF agents were killed.

Poor Judy was at home worrying, but thanks to that trooper, I was able to connect with her. I told her I was having a bad hair day and that Steve did not make it. I assured her I was OK and promised to talk to her soon.

ASAC Chuck was gone. As soon as we arrived at the intersection, he got into a vehicle and headed back to the command post. Many of the team leaders had been wounded and taken off to the hospital. We all just waited there for a while, not having any instructions on what to do next.

About 20 minutes later a school bus arrived. We got on the bus, and a female agent sitting two seats in front of me started rocking and saying over and over again, "This crap's not supposed to happen."

I walked over to her and patted her on the back. I said, "It's all right. We're getting the hell out of here."

Not Quite Finished

The bus took us about a mile away from the compound to a little lodge overlooking a small lake. Someone said it was the Fraternal Order of Police Lodge, and others said it was the Rotary or Kiwanis club lodge.

We got inside to find it had only a few chairs, so we all sat against the wall. One of the agents came in with a flash bang with its pin pulled.

"Does anybody have an extra pin?" he asked as he walked around the cabin.

"Put one of our flex cuffs around the flash bang," I said as I walked up to him. "That will hold the spoon down. Then put it outside and try not to set it off as you might get shot!"

I then sat down against the wall just trying to take in all that happened. Seemingly out of nowhere one of the support staff agents came up to us and handed us green Army socks and two boxes of 9 mm ammo. I took both even though I had not fired my weapon.

I hadn't fired for two reasons. First, I never acquired a target and second I did not want to waste ammunition. I did not know how long it would be before we were getting out of there.

I was startled when a couple of officers from the Waco SRT and Austin SRT Departments walked into the lodge. As soon as the gunfight began, reinforcements were called in from across Texas. One of their team members said, "We are gonna go in there and kill every one of those mother f'ers."

I Like the Idea, but Don't They Know What We Just Went Through?

The National Guard had provided us with an armored vehicle that was kept on standby. The initial plan was to run the personnel carrier straight through the compound and take the whole thing down if necessary. Word must have spread about the .50 caliber weapons, and the leadership team recognized that the armored plating on this vehicle would not stop a .50 caliber round.

Undeterred, they ordered up a second one, but as this armored vehicle was on its way, it broke down. All operations were then called off and it was decided we'd implement a containment strategy. I was very thankful for that.

We were driven back to the staging area, where we collected our vehicles and went to a local hotel. I'll never forget how good it felt to sit in a car seat as I drove to the hotel. When I got there, I went inside to check in.

At the front desk was one of the agent's wives. She had driven from Houston and was screaming at the front desk clerk demanding to know where her husband was. Of course he had no information.

"Who are you looking for?" I asked as I walked up to her.

After her reply, I told her he was on his way to the hotel and she shouldn't talk to the clerk anymore.

"Just wait here for your husband," I said. "If he's not here within an hour, call me in my room and I will help you."

Once I got into the room I went to the bathroom and I remember looking into the mirror and saying, "Holy crap."

Not sure what to do next, I began cleaning my equipment for later that night or the next day. Then I called and talked to Judy. I shared with her the news about Steve and the other agents who were killed and wounded that day. It was a sad call.

We were instructed to call in that evening, and that's when we were told to report the next morning. Wondering what the next day would bring, I took a shower, got dressed and went down to my car.

I was contemplating whether to go to the hospital to visit the wounded or just go to the drugstore, get some Tylenol PM and call it a day. When I got to the parking lot, I ran into an older agent named Nick.

"You want to go grab some dinner?" I asked.

"Yeah. I could use a drink," he said.

I reminded him that a couple of weeks earlier, in one of our training sessions, they warned us that having a drink after an extremely stressful situation made you more likely to become an alcoholic.

We both laughed and Nick said in a heavy southern accent, "It's for medicinal purposes only."

First, we made a stop at the hospital. There I saw the agent who was shot and lying in front of me. I was told he had no blood pressure when the medics got to him. He had been a medic for the El Paso Fire Department and his training served him well. As he was losing blood, he ended up lying down on the ground and elevated his feet. He saved his own life.

He was in his hospital room with his wife. I asked him, "Did you hear me yell at you to put mud on it?"

"I heard you yelling something, but I couldn't understand it," he said with a smile.

At least one of the Davidians was known to work at the hospital. There was some uncertainty about whether or not the Davidians would try to attack the hospital to get medical supplies for their wounded. No one was sure of how many people at the compound were hit or killed.

The Waco SRT team decided to guard the hospital for the evening. I asked the agent if he wanted my five shot revolver for his hospital room. He said no since he was severely sedated!

Nick and I went to the Circle K diner in Waco, and while we were eating CNN was on the television. CNN was showing news clips from the day's action. As images of the gun battle flickered across the screen, you could hear the restaurant patrons saying, "Where was this? Where in Waco?"

During dinner, Nick told me the story of what he did that day. He was carrying a sledgehammer in case we needed to break down a barrier once inside the compound. When the gunfire began, Nick was so caught up in the moment he held the sledgehammer like a rifle and tried to shoot it. He told me that after he put it up on his shoulder he quickly threw it on the ground while yelling, "Shiiiiiiiiiiiiiit!"

We went back to the hotel room. I phoned down to the front desk to set up my wakeup call and went to bed. My last thought of a very long day was, "What's going to happen tomorrow?"

Chapter 6

THE AFTERMATH

What Just Happened?

Before I went to bed, I checked in with the command post to find out what the plan was for the next day. We were instructed to meet the next morning in the technical college's gymnasium at 7:00 a.m. Once inside, all the agents sat on bleachers pulled out from the wall on one side of the old gym.

It appeared the gymnasium was built in the early 50's and was very small. Standing in front of us with SAC Phil was Daniel Hartnett, ATF's Associate Director of Law Enforcement, the agency's number two guy and Daniel Conroy, ATF Deputy Associate Director of Law Enforcement, the number three guy.

Hartnett began talking about how proud he was of our actions, and then one of the agents yelled out, "How come we did not have any AR-15s? Why were they given to the IRS?"

Hartnett really didn't have an answer for that, and another agent said, "This is bull crap."

And then another agent stood up, and another, and another—each demonstrating the anger building up inside of them. I could tell the agents were getting highly agitated and could feel the pressure in the room directly focused on Hartnett. It was clear the reaction stunned Hartnett. What he did next was pretty amazing. Without any warning he quickly yelled, "Let's have a moment of silence for our fallen agents!"

As soon as the moment of silence was finished he ran out of the gymnasium. How pathetic.

Harnett and Conroy arrived in Waco late in the day on the 28th. Once word got back to D.C. that a gunfight was underway, they headed south as quickly as possible. According to the official reports, they arrived at the ATF command post to find it in total disarray. It was a short time later, we would learn, they ceded command of the operation over to the FBI.

After the agents gathered in the gym, our team met briefly just outside the command post on the technical college campus. The first one to speak was SAC Phil. He told us how his helicopter was forced to land because it took fire.

He then told us that when he returned to the command post, he called the governor of Texas, Ann Richards. According to him, she said, "I am not going to give you anything to help kill Texans."

I was kind of taken aback by this statement. SAC Phil went on to say he was stunned by the phone conversation he had with the governor. He continued his efforts to get additional support for us while the gun battle raged on. Within one hour the head of the Texas Department of Public Safety called SAC Phil and told him he would send whatever support he needed.

Then ASAC Chuck spoke to us and apologized, saying he would never have sent us in if he knew this was going to happen. He started to break down and told us that he loved us, and never thought or knew this would happen.

Our team leaders then broke us up into our individual teams, and gave us assignments. My first assignment was to walk out to an intersection some 25 feet from the entrance of the technical college and guard the entrance of the command center. Later that day, our leaders moved us out onto the roads in front of the Davidian compound to perform perimeter duty.

While we were at our guard station, an agent came up to us in his G-ride and handed out AR-15s with one clip of ammo. The AR-15 I received, of course, was damaged. I could not get the bolt inside the rifle to slide back. Something was bent.

This kind of freaked me out, because as I was desperately trying to straighten the bolt, someone pulled up to a nearby mobile home located on the side of the road and ran inside. We spotted this, called it in and were told to see who was in the trailer. At the time, we did not know if the trailers were part of the compound or not.

I walked up to the trailer with two other agents. I told them my AR-15 did not work, so another agent went up to the door, banged on it and yelled, "Police! Come out."

There was no answer.

We called the situation in and asked if we were to make entry. We didn't hear anything for a few minutes and finally received a response saying, "Don't worry about it, they're okay." We later found out that these people were cleared at another checkpoint.

We had just finished that conversation when a car started coming toward us at a high rate of speed. We simultaneously aimed our rifles at the fast moving vehicle when the driver stopped about 50 yards from us and jumped out of the car. It was a DEA agent coming to the area to help us. He had gotten lost. What a relief!

Our cars were blocking the road, and I remember sitting there when our team leader walked up to us.

"How is everyone doing?" he asked.

"Fine," we replied in unison.

"Good. I wanted to let you know that you'll soon be moving," he said.

I was sitting on the road behind the car when he told us we were supposed to be a moving roadblock and patrolling the area.

"DiBetta, stay behind a minute," he said to me, "we'll be moving down the road shortly."

He then left with the two other agents and their cars. I was still sitting in the road all by myself for the first time – just thinking how this whole deal sucked. A few hours later we were relocated to a more permanent roadblock. There didn't appear to be any real strategy behind our activities.

It was getting late in the day and the agents were being sent back to the hotels, when I received a page from our command post. I got on the radio and was told to report to the command post. All I wanted to do was go back to the hotel room to sleep after another long day.

When I arrived at the command post, SAC Phil met me. He told me to get a locksmith so I could remove the G-rides of the agents who had died; the cars were still parked at the briefing site.

"How many vehicles are there?" I asked.

"Three."

"Do you have a phone book?" I asked, figuring that was a good place to start.

"No, but there may be one in there," he said pointing to the other room.

I began calling locksmiths and after several tries was finally able to get one. I told him I had three locked vehicles and gave him the location at which he was to meet me.

My next step was to ask for two more agents and another person to drive me to the briefing site to pick up the vehicles. When we arrived, the locksmith was waiting for us. I remember seeing just those three vehicles in the large open field that had been used as a parking lot.

It felt morbid. One of the vehicles was Steve's and another was a van used by the New Orleans SRT. It was clear that we moved out in a huge rush on the morning of the 28th, as the van was unlocked and inside was a new, fully loaded, double-burst, MP-5 in plain sight.

I secured the weapon and in about an hour and a half we were finished. We drove the vehicles up to the command post. I told Phil about the firearm I recovered and was told to take it to the agents who were standing guard at the hospital in case the Davidians showed up.

From Bad to Worse

In the following days and weeks, it became clear ATF was not handling the post-operation pressure any better than it did the operation itself. ATF's first misstatement to the media was the response that we did not lose the element of surprise. Clearly we had. Not only were the Davidians waiting for us, but on the 28th ASAC Chuck told us at the briefing sight we'd lost our surprise before even boarding the trailers.

I think Hartnett quickly gave over the responsibility of this whole operation to the FBI because he saw this as a no-win situation for us as an agency. ATF's senior management was increasingly worried about our actions in the field and the possibility of some agents retaliating against the Davidians.

Regardless of what happened, good or bad, he thought ATF's image was tainted and would no longer be an effective part of the investigation. When the agents learned of this, we were ticked off. It made us feel as though he thought we were so unprofessional we would do something like that! It was disappointing, but you could see his point.

The next day, ATF decided to have us gather by teams to receive peer support. Peer support was to bring together officers who had previously experienced a traumatic situation with officers who were recently in a traumatic situation. So they were here to help us get through a stressful time, and to talk to us about some of the feelings we would be experiencing after such an event.

That morning the agents were gathered into a big conference room on the campus. Then in walked our peer support contractor, a guy named Dr. Solomon. Solomon and some agent in the newly formed ATF peer group, talked to us for a few minutes before I noticed each of the tables had tissue boxes on them.

That's when they started telling us it was okay to cry, and if we wanted to cry we should go ahead and do it. They kept telling us this over and over again.

This is a bunch of crap. I remember starting to get a little ticked off about it. Then one of the peer support agents came up to me and said, "How do you feel?"

"Fine." I knew him from my time in New York. He was the one who liked to send me up the fire escapes.

"DiBetta, what would you do if a Davidian was trying to kill you?"

"I'd kill them first."

The agent seemed okay with that and walked on to someone else. To me, this was pretty much a big waste of our time.

The agents stationed in the hospital shared with me that when the peer support people came around to talk to them, they were also informed it was okay to cry. What I found odd was then the wounded agents were told how much worker's compensation money they could get for their injuries.

I felt really let down at this point by the way our agency was handling this. At no point were the agents given a sense of what we could expect in the future and there was virtually no follow up.

Another tidbit I did not find out until later was one of the reasons ATF was so adamantly repeating it had not lost the element of surprise. Apparently, Dr. Solomon talked to the ATF undercover agent, Robert, the one who walked into the Davidian compound the morning before the warrant was served. Dr. Solomon reported to ATF management that in his discussion with Robert, the agent told him ATF still held the element of surprise.

First of all, Dr. Solomon broke the doctor-patient privilege by disclosing that information. Robert later sued him for that breach of confidence and won the case. As a penalty resulting from this lawsuit, Dr. Solomon was to never again practice in the state of Texas. This just added more insult to the agents serving that day.

But more importantly, Robert himself told me that he had never said the element of surprise was not lost. He also told me he confirmed with ASAC Chuck during the phone conversation on the morning of the 28th that the Davidians knew ATF was coming. You may re-call even the sniper, who overheard Robert's conversation in the U/C house, started packing his gear after hearing that conversation.

The following day, March 3, a memorial service was held in a Waco church. It was surrounded by news media trying to get pictures of us as we were entering. There was no respect for anyone's privacy. As I walked past the cameras, I scratched my face with my middle finger—thus ensuring I would not be on the local news. Without moving my mouth, I walked by and said, "A-holes." I know it was not the most mature thing to do, but I was just so angry at the media for letting the Davidians know we were coming.

The media was also getting hostile towards both the ATF and FBI. They were upset the local news media vehicle, which was involved in tipping off the Davidians of our arrival, was accidentally run over by one of the FBI's armored vehicles. It should also be noted the news media who were out there on the morning of the 28th had illegal scan-ners and were listening to cellular phone calls as well. There was talk of charging them for using an illegal wiretap, but nothing ever became of it.

Heading Home

Finally, on Thursday, March 4, it was announced that we could go home after the day's shift. I started packing up my gear when I received a page. I called the command post and was told to report there. I arrived at the command post and SAC Phil was there to meet me.

He told me to take Steve Willis' death certificate and the personal effects from his vehicle back to Houston. Once I was there, I was to contact the agent assigned to assist Steve's parents in their time of loss. I drove back in a caravan with three other agents. It was dark out on the country roads and couldn't see anything for miles except for the road and the cars in front of me. I remember how much I was looking forward to going to sleep in my own bed. Later that night, Judy and I attended Steve Willis' viewing, and I dropped off the death certificate. It was a very sad day. Former President George H.W. Bush attended the viewing, and the funeral was well attended by law enforcement agen-cies from across the state. I placed a small ATF badge in the coffin with Steve at the end of the viewing.

At ATF a fund was established among agents. Each agent puts in $20 a year and if you were killed, your designee would receive a $25,000 check. Steve had never updated his designee, so it ended up being split between his parents and an old girlfriend he hadn't seen in years. When the agents went to deliver the check, she was mortified and tried to refuse it. The agents finally convinced her to accept it and do whatever she wanted with it.

After Steve's funeral, I went home and slept for the entire weekend. I don't think I was ever so tired in my life. I don't remember eating or using the bathroom. I just slept. Monday came and I felt like my head was going to explode. I got a call from ASAC Donnie and he told me I had to go into the office. I asked if I could have another day off and he said, "No." I had to go in, nobody else was there. I went to the office and took about four aspirin just so I could think clearly.

By now, things were not looking too good for us in the press. ATF had lousy spokespeople. The truth was coming out about the element of surprise. ASAC Donnie, who was born and raised in Mississippi, would start to speak with a heavy Mississippi accent when he got nervous. This did not come across very well during TV interviews. It was so bad that people started calling the ATF's division office, and saying, "Now we know why you guys screwed up so bad in Waco. You have idiots for bosses!"

Sadly, that was one of the nice comments!

When I got into the office that morning, one of the administrative assistants came up to me almost in tears, and said, "Dave, can you please take these phone calls?"

The administrative assistants were fearful of answering the phones because of the language and the threats being made. A little while later, ASAC Donnie came into the office and told me our radio system in Waco was all messed up and it had to be fixed.

"What's wrong with it?" I asked him.

"I don't know. Just get it fixed," he replied.

I'd only been in the office for an hour and still hadn't gotten to my 30 phone messages. I didn't even look at my pager, and even my new e-mail mailbox was loaded, too!

I called our radio tech to find out what was going on with the radios. After speaking with him, I discovered the problem. The signal repeater in Austin was Daisy-linked to the system in Waco. After an incident like this, where we still didn't have a full accounting of all our equipment, we had to change the radio code. The only way to get that done was to have the Austin field office do it.

When I called Austin, I spoke with an administrative assistant and asked her who was in charge. She told me it was, Don, the same guy in charge of the agents at the U/C house and the one who was snoring the night before we served the warrant.

"Don, you have to replace the code to make the radio system work in Waco," I said to him.

"Dave, don't you understand we've been in a gun battle?" he replied, as though I wasn't even there.

"It doesn't matter," I said. "You have to change the code now. This is your top priority, nothing else matters," I said with a bit more conviction.

He started getting really testy with me, so I told him to let me know when the radio code was changed. I think that was last time I ever spoke with him.

He left a message that afternoon with our administrative assistant, saying the job was done.

Then, I think the crazies woke up, because I started getting a lot of phone calls from people complaining about our management. Again, I thought my head was going to explode. It was almost like you had to repeat the same thing over and over again.

The worst part was I never even saw any of the news clips to which these people were reacting. I began watching the news, and the stations were now doing voiceovers on ASAC Donnie. That seemed to quell the calls almost immediately.

That same day, I also had to make arrangements to return Steve's items to his father. I ended up talking to the agent assigned to Steve's dad, told him what I had and left my number with him. When Steve's dad finally got back with me, I told him what I had and he said, "Make sure there's nothing in there that would embarrass his mother."

I had to laugh, because if you knew Steve, he was never without a girlfriend. Several showed up at his funeral. I made arrangements with the agent to turn over all of Steve's items. I also told the agent to collect any ATF equipment, like radios, chargers, etc. He said he would.

For a while, every day brought new issues needing to be addressed. You could see ASAC Donnie was not up to the task. Here's an example:

Whenever there is a personnel change, for any reason, locks to the office have to be changed. Steve's death was no exception. The locks to Steve's office were changed, and I was given the new key to be placed in the SAC's safe.

I went up to ASAC Donnie to give him the key. He got highly agitated and said, "I don't need the stupid key."

"Donnie, it's for the safe," I said.

"What do you mean?"

"The SAC has a key to all offices for two reasons: in case there is an emergency, and if internal affairs wants to get into the office."

"I don't care. You keep the key," he said.

Another time we had to rekey a secure phone in the office and needed the key from the safe. It then became clear why he was getting so upset. He'd either lost the combination, or did not receive it from SAC Phil. It ended up costing us $700 to get the safe opened.

ASAC Donnie was also upset about the number of magazines we were getting. SAC Phil was an avid reader. ASAC Donnie would come back to our office, throw the magazines in a chair, and say, "Why am I still getting this stuff? I want it to stop now."

Instead of telling his administrative assistant to stop giving him the magazines and let the subscriptions expire, he made a big production out of this.

I do not know if it was his management style, or his insecurity in the position. I guess I'll never know. I thought he'd be a little better towards me, especially after an incident a few weeks earlier when they brought in all the wives of the agents involved in Waco. Donnie started talking and the women were already highly agitated. They started going after him, asking, "How could you let our husbands get into this situation?"

My wife was the only one who stood up for him and said to the wives, "You know, your husbands are in dangerous jobs and anything could happen. Unfortunately it did."

It was becoming increasing clear that SAC Phil and ASAC Chuck were not coming back in the next couple of months. We lost Associate Director Hartnett, as well as Director Stevens, and when the new director, a guy named Magaw from Secret Service arrived, he wanted both of them fired immediately.

I guess due to his lack of experience, he did not realize without civil service due process, Chuck and Phil could not be fired. They probably did, however, have one of the longest administrative leaves ever. Because of how they were fired, they were both able to return to ATF. Phil became a liaison with U.S. Customs.

Donnie told us not to speak to Phil unless instructed to. So, he just sat at his desk over at Customs. I believe that went on for a couple of years before he retired.

Chuck, on the other hand, had a little more time before he could receive his pension. He was placed in the visual information branch as a non-agent, but as the chief in our D.C. Headquarters. He also received a car, which, by the way, I purchased! That story comes later on in the book.

Feelings, Emotions and Questions

On March 8, 1993, ATF finally had a psychologist who knew what he was talking about speak with us. He was the Houston Police Department's contracted psychologist, and was a very interesting person.

He went through the standard emotions that one would experience while going through a traumatic incident. Then he began telling us stories, and one in particular stays in my mind. He talked of a Houston police officer killed in the line of duty who had a wonderful funeral with full honors. As part of their support, the Houston Police Department arranged to have this psychologist speak with the surviving spouse.

The wife of the deceased officer said that he was an ass, was not a very good husband, and was planning to file for divorce before he was killed. The spouse went on to say she felt such guilt because she did not like her husband. And it was interesting what the Houston police psychologist said to this woman.

"Everybody goes through grief after a tragic incident differently."

He told us, "Some of you will be angry about this incident for the rest of your life. Some will let it fade in your memory, and still others could let this incident ruin your life."

It was probably the first sound advice we received.

That first psychologist was just telling us to cry, and a lot of us didn't feel that way. At least this guy made you feel like whatever emotion you had was okay and you did not have to feel one particular way or another. He also told us to "try not to drink too much." This made everybody laugh and then he said, "Get a lot of rest."

I want to take a minute to talk about guilt. After an event like this, you always have that overriding guilt. You question yourself and wonder if you could have done something better, or if there was anything you did to make things worse. The worst part about those questions is there never is an answer. What was done is done, and the things you could've done differently and their effect on an outcome, you'll never know.

A few weeks later, acting SAC Donnie was fully in charge of the division now, and the office received two new ASAC's. A few weeks after serving the warrant, I asked for a couple of days off. In our manual orders, it says that if an agent is involved in a shooting he's allowed three administrative days for personal time.

I asked Donnie if I could have my three admin days and he told me, "No." This surprised me, so I told him what was in the manual orders.

"I don't care, and if you put in for the time off, I won't sign it," he said.

When the day came for me to take my previously requested administrative leave, I did. I documented it on my timesheets as such and no one ever said a word to me. I'm sure that endeared me to Donnie a little bit more, and the relationship just continued to go downhill.

During the 51 days of the FBI's siege of the compound, I made several trips to Waco as the TOO. There was always a lot of activity. You never knew what was going to happen. For example, the FBI wanted to cut power to the Davidians. The FBI decided to shoot out the transformer, telling only their Hostage Rescue Team, but not their negotiation team or other law enforcement personnel. So when they shot out the transformer, everybody was on high alert and hit the dirt!

Some of the agents were taking helicopter rides, and at one point the helicopter was flying so low it hit some power lines. This was a bad thing! You could tell the snipers were nervous. They fortified their positions with one layer of sandbags followed by a half-inch metal plate with a cutout to put a rifle through, and then four more layers of sandbags. They were worried about that .50 caliber.

When I went up there, I tried to gather as much ATF equipment as I could. Some of the lenses were worth thousands of dollars and were being tossed around. Nobody realized what they were, or who owned them.

During the time of the siege, some of the off-duty agents would go to the hotel bar to have a beer. Since Waco was a small town and there was limited hotel space, news crews and reporters would frequent the same bars as the agents. It was pretty easy to distinguish who was who.

The news reporters would always try to send beer to the agents, hoping that if they had a few beers, their tongues would loosen up. One of the agents told me he loved this tactic because all the while he drank for free and never gave out any information. The agents were under orders from ATF management not to speak to the press for any reason, but it didn't stop the anonymous sources from telling the truth about the element of surprise.

On March 11, 1993, every agent involved in serving the warrant was sent to Fort Fisher. Fort Fisher is in Waco and is home to the Texas Ranger's museum. They took us in one-at-a-time to get statements about what happened the day we served the warrant. We were shown drawings of the compound and asked to identify the locations from which we took fire, what steps we took, our placement in the trailers and what Davidians, if any, we contacted. This process lasted about an hour.

The Siege Ends

On April 19, the Davidian compound burned to the ground. I was on my third day of administrative leave and while at home I had the TV on. I was taking delivery of kitchen cabinets as I watched the news develop. I was standing with the delivery man watching the compound burn. I know this is wrong of me, but when the compound was fully engulfed, the image brought me a sense of relief. In my mind, that place was nothing but sadness, between the alleged child abuses, credit card fraud, manipulation of his religion, etc., the list could go on and on. I was just happy it was over.

By now the press coverage of the event was hostile. The press believed they were not being treated properly by the federal agencies, and were frustrated because they were not getting anywhere buying beer for the agents at night in the local bars. There was very little reporting or statements in the media about whether or not the Davidians were firing on the FBI when the compound was burning.

After the event, I saw several pictures of Davidians who had burned to a crisp while lying in the prone position with rifles in their hands beside a pile of ammunition. The FBI agents who were on the ground said they were under constant fire and exposed themselves numerous times trying to save those Davidians trying to escape.

It was also clear from the tapes made through the listening devices inside the compound, that the Davidians were pouring kerosene in the upper hallways of the compound. The compound sat on higher ground in an open field with acres and acres of low brush surrounding it. When the FBI was trying to inject the non-explosives teargas into the building, it opened up air holes, so now you have the compound on the high ground with a lot of open air holes for oxygen to feed the fire. The Davidians were spreading the accelerant on the dry wood. Remember, the compound was built with used material from houses that were more than 20 years old. It didn't take long for the fire to consume that structure.

During the investigation that followed, it was found the FBI did shoot a single round from an M203 grenade launcher that was capable of generating heat, but they only used it on the left side of the compound near the bunker and it landed on the mud floor. This was done because the tanks being used to insert the gas could not get into that lower level of the compound.

A U.S. attorney who worked on this case got fired because that was in the final report and he removed it. I have no idea why he would do that. The truth always comes out in the end.

When the compound was on fire, there were large explosions. I believe these were likely to be from the compound's fuel supply, as well as the large amount of ammunition the Davidians had in the building. There were always questions regarding the lack of fire trucks on standby. To me, the answer to those questions was simple. The tanks were taking a ton of fire. With the standoff range you needed, because of the .50 caliber machine gun, there was no way a fire truck could be put within a mile of the compound without endangering the lives of the firemen.

Also, live ammunition was cooking off and firing in all directions as the fire consumed the compound. Some of the Davidians came out of the building with their homemade grenades, believing this was the end in which would all die in a huge blaze and get resurrected again with David Koresh as the Messiah and the Davidians as his disciples.

I read from the autopsy reports that it was clear Koresh was in a kneeling position while someone shot him in the head, and his number two guy, Schroeder, also had a self-inflicted gunshot wound to the head. The saddest part was that some of the children were inside a small bunker at the entrance to the house and when the fire got going many died from asphyxiation, while others perished from exposure to the explosions. At the command post, it was a very solemn site, especially at the processing area for the children. It was loaded with donated toys that would never be used.

After the fire, the state of Texas and the Department of Justice tried to determine who would investigate the fire scene. The only agency on the federal level with this type of expertise was ATF, but that was not going to happen due to the perceived prejudices any ATF report would generate.

It was decided to go to the state fire investigators, and one of the better fire investigators was in Houston. The problem was, not only did he work with ATF on the arson task force, he also was married to an ATF administrative assistant. He was selected anyway, because of his expertise and national recognition as a cause and origin expert.

Based on all the physical evidence, including the audiotapes, it was clear the Davidians set the fire themselves. I remember there was talk about trying to sue the federal government over the cause of the fire, but after the report came out, no lawsuits were successfully brought against the government.

Off to Court

It was decided to move the court proceedings for the surviving Davidians to San Antonio, Texas. After the 51-day standoff, and all the publicity, Waco was too small of an area from which to draw an unbiased jury.

ATF set up a small command post at Fort Sam Houston and had the witnessing agents report there for trial preparation. I was assigned to go up there and assist the U.S. Marshals.

U.S. Marshals were in charge of court security. They were from New Orleans as were the tech agents they brought with them. The senior Marshal was adamant about not having any trouble at this trial.

I told him we were there to support him in any way needed. One of the tech agents shared that they called him, "dirt boy."

When one of the agents called him that, I asked him, "What did you say?"

"I called him dirt boy," he replied.

As a teenager, Dave was active in Boy Scouts of America, here shown after earning the rank of Eagle Scout.

During basic training in Alabama, 1984.

On the Beach at Fort Miles, Delaware, as military Policeman.

Dave served three months overseas on military exercises, looking out on a balcony in Germany.

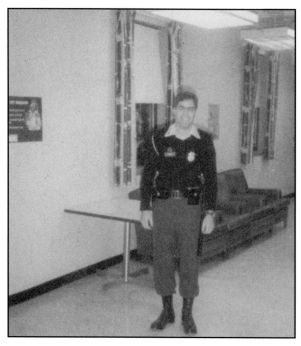

Military police garrison uniform at Fort Meade, Maryland; getting ready for patrol.

Prior to joining ATF, Dave served with the U.S. Customs Services, and is pictured here at the U.S. Border Inspection station, Glynco, Georgia

Standard Form 46 Revised Jan. 1977 USCSC FPM Chapter 930	U.S. Government Motor Vehicle Operator's Identification Card		Card No. LE:NY:104	
Name of Operator			Sex	Date Issued
DIBETTA David			M	1/4/88
Height	Weight	Date of Birth	Social Security No.	Date Expires
5'10"168				1/4/90

Color of

NOT TRANSFERABLE
Card must be carried at all times when operating Government vehicles.

Signature of Operator (*Not valid until signed*)

Hair	Eyes
BR	BR

Name and Location of Issuing Unit
Bureau of ATF
90 Church St.
New York, N.Y.10007

Signature and Title of Issuing Official
Special Agent In Charge 264-4658

The holder of this card is qualified to operate U.S. Government vehicles and/or equipment specified, subject to the restrictions set forth on the reverse of this card.

46-105

Above and below, government motor vehicle license issued in NYC, so we would not get tickets!

Restrictions None - Not valid for non-Gov't owned vehicles

QUALIFIED TO OPERATE

Type Vehicle and/or Equipment	Capacity	Qualifying Official
Auto/Light Trucks - The vehicle operated by this driver is self insured and owned by the U.S. Gov't. Current registration is available.		

OTHER RECORDS (*Optional*)
For further information or valida-tion, contact Bureau of Alcohol, Tobacco & Firearms (212) 264-4657.

☆ U.S. GOVERNMENT PRINTING OFFICE : 1981 O - 361-526 (7159)

AN... ...THORIZED TO CAR... ...R ARMS, EXE-CUTE ... ...TS, MAKE ARRESTS ... ...FFENSES AGAINST ... ...NITED STATES AND TO ...RFORM SUCH OTHER D...TI...S AS AUTHORIZED BY LAW.

DIRECTOR

No. SA2740

SIGNATURE OF BEARER

Picture of original ATF ID, taken January 4, 1988.

SRT Training – repelling the five-story practice tower in Texas.

SRT Training – setting up on a stack before making entry

SRT Training – our team before night maneuvers

SRT Training – getting pepper sprayed

SRT Training – running obstacle course

That's Dave navigating the obstacle course at SRT training in Alabama.

Dave (back center) and other Texas ATF agents, just after his arrival to Houston in December 1989.

In front of the trailers with SRT members the day before serving the warrant on the Branch Davidians. The photo was taken February 27, 1993.

Radio checks in communication vans a few days before Waco.

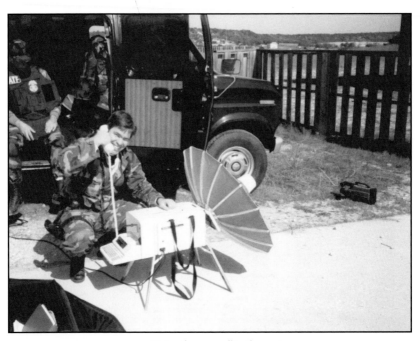

Testing the new satellite phone.

Cattle trucks used during training to carry agents to the compound.

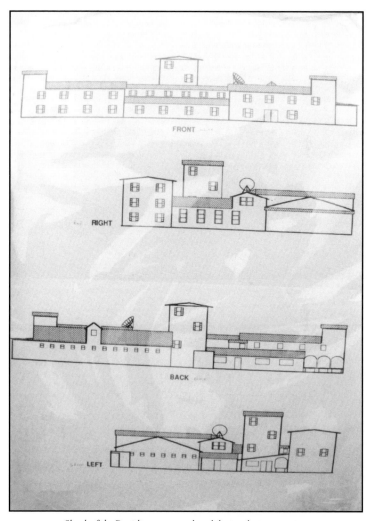

Sketch of the Davidian compound used during the investigation.

Aerial photo of the compound the day after the warrant was served. Note the cattle cars are in the same position as the previous day.

This underground school bus was part of the bunker complex at the Waco compound. It was used as a firing range placed underground to muffle the sound of gun fire.

The sniper tower disguised as a water tower.

Insider the sniper tower…this medal ladder led to several sniper landings.

Several motorcycles seized at the Waco compound, with David Koresh's customized bike in the middle.

Gas tank art displayed on David Koresh's motorcycle…
he was obviously a big fan of Madonna.

Seized car of a Branch Davidian member who also worked for the US Postal Service. The local news media inadvertantly tipped-off the Davidians of the upcoming warrant when they told the driver to avoid the area.

The undercover house used by ATF.

Underground bunker access assigned to Dave as seen following the siege after the Texas Rangers dug out the entrance. Note the sniper tower in the background (right), which kept him from leaving the ditch.

Close-up shot of the entrance to the underground bunker.

Dave manning a post in the days after serving the warrant.

Dave (left) and Harry, the agent who pulled Dave out of the muddy hole he used when he came under fire while serving the warrant at the compound.

21-gun salute by the Texas State Trooper Honor Guard

FBI sniper position set up at the undercover house.

Dave and another agent standing by the flagpole at the Branch Davidian compound.

A local rancher posted this sign thanking the ATF and other agencies for their service in Waco.

The OV-10 Bronco. This plane was used for aerial observance at Waco.

Following the seige at Waco, waving in the breeze at half-mast are the American, State of Texas, and ATF flags.

1996 Atlanta Olympic Games with the Olympic mascot.

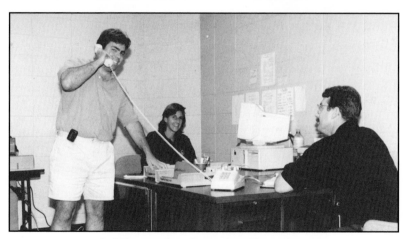

At ATF command post during Atlanta Olympic Games.

Texas Special Olympics

Texas Special Olympics

T-shirt given to Dave at his going away party in Texas; "Get outta here..." a phrase he used often!

Plaque recieved at the same celebration.

Dave receiving the Distinguished Service Medal from ATF Director Magaw.

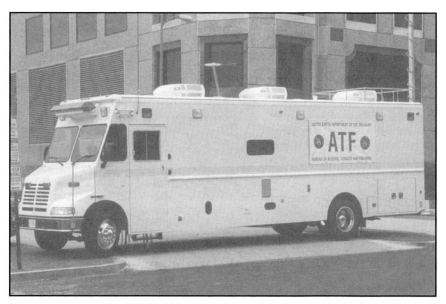

ATF's Mobile Command Post (MCP), which arrived in January 1998. Dave helped design this upgraded vehicle.

Dave with Senator Joe Biden while a FLEOA representative, 1999.

Senator Joe Biden with FLEOA officers during his speech at the FLEOA Chapter 38 Luncheon, ca. August 2001. Pictured from l-r: Chapter 38 Treasurer SA Bob Delgado (IRS), Chapter Vice President Kurt Hansen (USMS), Senator Joe Biden, Chapter 38 President David DiBetta (ATF), FLEOA ATF Agency President Art Gordon, FLEOA member SA Diane Lardella (ATF), and FLEOA National President Rich Gallo.

Doing a sound check prior to the 15th Anniversary of Waco Memorial Service.

FLEOA ATF Agency President Dave DiBetta at the ATF Memorial Service honoring four ATF agents killed in the line of duty. Photo courtesy of The Eighteen Eleven, the journal of the Federal Law Enforcement Officers Association.

Bench that memorializes ATF Special Agents Steven Willis, Robert Williams, Conway LeBleu and Todd McKeehan who lost their lives February 28, 1993, in the line of duty. As president of the FLEOA ATF Agency, Dave was instrumental in getting the memorial bench placed.

The ATF robot developed in the late 1990s.

THURSDAY, JULY 30, 2009 ••• THE NEWS JOURNAL B9

Kaufman honors retiring ATF agent from Delaware

Senator praises those who serve the public

By NICOLE GAUDIANO
Gannett Washington Bureau

WASHINGTON — As a member of a law enforcement advocacy group, Middletown resident Dave DiBetta worked with Joe Biden in the Senate last year to pass legislation honoring law enforcement officers for their bravery.

On Wednesday, it was DiBetta's turn to be honored when the vice president's replacement in the Senate, Ted Kaufman, paid tribute to his nearly three decades of federal service. That includes almost 22 years as a special agent with the U.S. Bureau of Alcohol, Tobacco, Firearms and Explosives.

DiBetta is among a dozen federal employees with commendable careers who have been honored by Kaufman. The senator spent 22 years as a federal employee himself, working for Biden when Biden represented Delaware in the Senate.

"Dave DiBetta's story is one of so many in Delaware and across the country," Kaufman said, standing near a poster-sized photo of DiBetta on the Senate floor. "His willingness to risk his own safety to serve the common good recalls the heroism of our revolutionary forebears, like Caesar Rodney, Thomas McKean and those Delawareans who were the first to vote for separation and who fought for freedom."

DiBetta, 49, will retire this year from the ATF Wilmington office, where he oversees tobacco and firearms investigations. Throughout his career, he has worked on high-risk missions, taught undercover investigation techniques, served as an air marshal and provided security for special events, including two national political conventions and the Olympics.

In 1993, he was one of the officers charged with serving warrants during the deadly siege at the Branch Davidian complex in Waco, Texas. The mission earned him the ATF's Distinguished Service Medal, and he has received other awards throughout his career.

DiBetta brought his wife, Judy, and five other family members to the Senate to hear Kaufman's tribute.

"I'm humbled by it," he said. "It's great being recognized for your achievements over your career."

Kaufman's honorees represent a variety of federal agencies, from the military to the National Institutes of Health. He has honored about one a week for the past few months.

In some cases, his office has worked with the Partnership for Public Service to identify them. He has met other honorees through staff members, including his chief of staff's father. He met DiBetta, the first Delawarean, last month at St. Anthony's Italian Festival in Wilmington.

After his speech, Sen. Chris Dodd, a Connecticut Democrat, praised Kaufman's focus on unsung federal employees who make a difference.

"For a relative newcomer and short-timer, you've made a substantial contribution to our country," Dodd said of Kaufman, who was appointed to replace Biden in the Senate and has said he won't run for election next year.

Kaufman plans to continue sharing such stories throughout his term.

"This has been a labor of love for me, talking about great federal employees," he said.

Contact Nicole Gaudiano at ngaudiano@gannett.com.

Delaware news journal

Senator Ted Kaufman with Dave following Kaufman's presentation on the senate floor, July 2009.

Dave cleaning his M-4 just prior to his retirement from ATF.

In Memory

SA Steven David Willis,
Dec. 18, 1960 - February 28, 1993.

SA Robert J. Williams,
March 1, 1966 - February 28, 1993.

SA Conway LeBleu,
1963 - February 28, 1993.

SA Todd W. McKeehan,
1965 - February 28, 1993.

"Why?"

"One time on a brutally hot day we were setting up some equipment underneath a house and had to dig under a particular area of the structure," he said. "While he was digging, the dirt collapsed around him and instead of asking for help when the agents were calling him, he said, 'I'd rather stay here in the dirt. It is nice and cool.' That's how he got his name dirt boy."

While we were at Fort Sam Houston in San Antonio to present our depositions, ATF made a big deal of it and were providing the agents with security using SRT members. On the day my name appeared on the witness list, I asked the head of the detail, "Where's my protection?"

"What do you mean?" he asked me.

"I'm on the witness list and I want my SRT protection," I said to him.

He checked the list and sure enough, my name was on it. Then he looked at me and said, "You don't need that."

I just start laughing and thought, It's not the mission, it's about the show.

I thanked the supervisor for his support and walked away. That must've ticked him off. I was removed from the witness list.

After the trial, in which all the Davidians were convicted, we were taken back to the compound for closure. We were transported in yellow school buses. As we proceeded through the community, it was nice to see the many signs the citizens put up thanking us for our service.

Upon arriving at the compound, I saw it was completely burnt down to the ground. There were flies everywhere. We received yellow boots to wear while walking around the compound due to the high level of contaminants at the scene.

I actually climbed up the tower were the one Davidian sniper was, and later learned he was shot in the chest and bled out right there. When I climbed up, I went through five levels using the small, attached ladder. When I reached the top level, there was still coagulated blood from the sniper on the platform.

I actually climbed to the top level and looked out through the hole from which he had been shooting. During the investigation, as they sifted for bullets, the dirt around the hole in the ground that provided me with shelter had been moved around. I could see I had been lucky. If the shooter would've concentrated a little bit more, he could've easily shot me. That was an unnerving feeling.

Later in the day, we also saw Koresh's personal motorcycle. He had airbrushed a heart and taped a picture of Madonna (the singer) on his gas tank. He had a crush on her. We saw the little bunker near the front door where all the women and children died, as well as where they buried their dead following the original shootout. The tunnel system through which I was supposed to enter that day was also unearthed. All I can say is, I'm glad we didn't make entry. It was a lot smaller and narrower than originally thought. Even with it completely burnt down, it was clear this was a huge complex.

There was a short memorial service. The Texas state troopers brought their honor guard, a chaplain said a prayer and then Taps was played. A strange thing happened as soon Taps began. It started to rain and the second he stopped playing, it stopped raining. It was almost like God was crying over this event. It was a moving ceremony.

Months later the trial and sentencing came. CNN had a huge interest in the story and bought a house to work in that was right by the courthouse. More and more I was hoping to get this all behind us, but then the hearings from Capitol Hill came.

The Missing Tape

There was a lot of talk about a videotape being made of ATF serving the warrant. Many thought it was important to determine who fired first. It was an issue for Democrats and Republicans, but no one could locate the tape. While the hearings were going on, I received a phone call from an investigator on one of the oversight committees.

The investigator said it was his understanding that I was the person to go to see about this tape that was made.

"Yeah," I replied to him, "Who made that statement?"

I could hear the papers rustling around in the background and he gave me the agent's name. It was John. The same agent who worked in the U/C house and had asked me how to use a tripod. He also was the agent who and had set up the camera before Robert was safely back in the house on the morning of the 28th.

"What does the statement say?" I asked him.

The investigator replied, "The agent said, 'I put the tape in the recorder and then I hit record.'"

"Did he say anything else after that?"

"No."

"I'll give John a call and let you know what I discover," I said.

I gave John a call, and luckily for me he answered right away.

"John, did you say in your Ranger report, that you put a tape into a VCR recorder and then pressed record, because you were supposed to be videotaping the execution of the warrant?"

"Yes."

"Haven't you followed the hearings? There's a big uproar about the tape, and they are saying there is a big government conspiracy in trying to hide the tape," I said. "What exactly happened that morning?"

"I put the tape in, hit record and then keyed the radio," he replied.

The term, "key the radio" is nothing more than squeezing the mike to press the talk button. When the radio is in that position, it's called a keyed mike, which also makes the radio transmit.

"The tape ejected," John went on to say

"Why did that happen?" I asked, knowing that the gear had been tested and the radio had not had an adverse affect on any of the other equipment.

"I moved the antenna from the closet to the top of the VCR so it was in front of the window, for better reception," he said.

"Then what happened?"

"The VCR stopped recording, and then ejected the tape."

"Why didn't you put that in your statement?"

I think he replied something along the lines of, "I didn't think it was as important."

"You're killing me," I said. "If I need any more information, I will call you right back."

I immediately got back on the phone with the investigator and told him what happened. He asked me the same question, "Why didn't he include that information in his report?"

I shared with him what John told me.

"Would you be able to re-create what he claims happened that day?" he asked me.

"We have a list of equipment that was used in the U/C house, including the VCR and the converter COM," I said. "If you give me an hour, I will try to re-create what happened that morning."

Fortunately for us, we had the VCR, and the converter COM used at the U/C house in our office. On our workbench, I set up the VCR and placed the converter COM's antenna on the VCR just like they did that day. I put the tape into the VCR and pressed record. I waited a minute so the machine went fully through its cycle and then I keyed the radio. The VCR turned off.

I tried this several times and the same thing happened. I also tried it as soon as the tape was put in and the same thing happened—the VCR turned off. I could not get it to eject.

The converter COM puts out a lot of energy and sometimes the silicon chips, like those in the VCR, reads that energy as a command and overrides its current action to shut off and possibly eject.

My theory was there probably were a couple more agents standing around, and your body has a high percentage of water, which reflects radio frequency energy. That probably gave it enough additional power to eject the tape that day. It did clearly show however, that it would disable the VCR when the radio mike was keyed.

I called the investigator and shared my findings.

"You're kidding," he said.

"No, sir, I'm not," I replied. "I will keep the equipment off to the side and not let anybody use it until you tell me otherwise."

That kind of quelled one of the great conspiracy theories that brewed up in Waco's aftermath. The agent should have given a more complete statement, even if it made him look bad. There was nothing wrong with the radio; he just didn't understand the concept of how it worked.

Seeing the Light on Waco

The hearings were great. Robert, the undercover agent who met Koresh on the day ATF served the warrant, actually called ASAC Chuck a liar. The evidence showed that Chuck's version of the events that day was skewed. Once the rest of the hundred-plus agents and police officers saw and heard what was presented, Chuck and others began to change their stories.

I believe somewhere in my papers is a memo from Chuck telling us how stress makes you forget certain facts. He claimed he was under a lot of stress that day, and that's what caused the factual inaccuracies in his statements.

Another SAC, Ted, who served in the command post, witnessed all the events of that day. He also had short-term memory loss, but after a 12-hour interview with ATF's internal affairs, he started to remember all the events of that day more clearly. He also changed his statement about how he could not hear anything about the pre-warrant discussions due to the helicopter engine noise, but in a video it showed the helicopter engine was not running. His revised testimony led him to write a memo, where in his opening paragraph he wrote, "I've seen the light and my memory came back."

How sad was that? After that, they sent him to EPIC in El Paso (El Paso Intelligence Center). That only lasted a few years and he ended up coming back to headquarters, where he ran the Intel division before he retired.

The hearings were unable to determine who in headquarters gave the green light for the operation to proceed. There was always a lot of speculation about that. When you're in a position like that, you usually defer to what the ground supervisor says, unless you see something obviously flawed in the plan.

During the hearings, David Thibodeau, a Davidian who survived the fire, testified. In his testimony, Thibodeau complained that when the warrant was being served, an ATF agent was yelling profanities at him. It was later shown that he was the one trying to get out of the bunker, but turned back when he realized I was there.

He also prided himself in saying he could've shot the ATF agent on the other side of the wall, but decided not to do it. Given the bunker's small opening, it would have been physically impossible for him to get a shot on me.

I became known as the unidentified agent swearing at the Davidians.

Even though this was a huge and tragic event affecting just about everyone in our division and our agency, the other work still needed to get done. We executed some 30-35 percent fewer high-risk warrants than before the Waco incident. It was funny, ATF wasn't very well known, but after Waco, everyone knew us. And everyone wanted to hear our story.

After this experience, and witnessing the manner in which ATF treated Robert and the rest of us involved, I decided to make myself financially sound. I had begun investing in real estate properties, but decided at this point to ramp up my investments. I felt uneasy about having to endure another investigation such as this one, and if ATF put me in that type of a situation again, I wanted to be set in case I had to quit.

Stories About Donnie

SAC Donnie was increasingly hostile to me and everyone else in the Division. The TOO shop just moved to a new space and I was setting up to do a firearms deal with a group when Donnie telephoned.

"I'm leaving the office in five minutes and I need a new battery for my pager," he said. "And I need you to figure out where the push cart is because another ATF group needs it to move evidence."

"I'll take care of it," I said.

I called one of the administrative assistants in his office—she sat directly across from Donnie—and asked if she could give him a battery for his pager because he was in a hurry to go to another meeting. I then started calling around to the different groups to figure out where the cart was. My intention was to drive over and get the cart and bring it to the office that needed it.

Just as I located the cart, I received another call. It was Donnie and he was irate.

"Why did this administrative assistant give me the battery when I told you to get me a battery?" he screamed.

"You told me you were in a hurry, you had to leave and I had to locate the cart, so I asked her to bring you the battery so you wouldn't be late," I replied not believing what I was hearing.

"I located the cart at your office and I'm on my way to pick it up," I added.

He went ballistic. He said he'd told me to get him the battery, not her, and on and on. He then told me he would no longer speak with me over the phone. Every time he had a question or wanted me to do something, I had to go to his office.

"I understand," I said.

The next day he called me to his office just to ask me a yes or no question. I got into my car and drove the five minutes to appear in front of him. This went on for a couple months. I guess he had to prove he was the boss.

From then on I just tried to avoid him as much as I could. I tried not to deal with him at all. Anytime I could get away with it, I would let his messages go to voicemail. On a weekend before a federal holiday, I was told by Donnie to go to Dallas to hook up a RDNR (remote dial number recorder) for a Dallas agent by the following Tuesday morning.

I had to travel from Houston to Dallas on that Monday, the holiday, and finalize all the work on Tuesday when everybody else returned from his or her day off. After I finished my work on Monday, I met with the agent.

"What's the problem with your tech agents that they weren't able to do this?' I asked him.

"I forgot to tell them to do this pen register, and the 10-day install order expires tomorrow morning," he said.

"What group are you in and where is the connection point being set up?" I asked.

"I don't have that information," he said.

"I'll call the phone company myself," I said disgustedly. "Can you tell me about the area we'll be working in?"

If it was a bad part of town, I'd want at least two other agents out there with me.

"I'm not sure, since I don't work in that area," he replied.

"So, why did you decide to put a tap way out there?"

"I'm doing it to help out another law enforcement agency," he said.

I think his lack of communication is the reason why his own Tech agents did not install the device, so I had to go up there to do it. I had the agent drive me to the location to set up the equipment. His car was fairly new, but the tires looked like they were about to fall off and had little to no air in them.

I pointed the situation out to him and he told me he hoped to trash the car, because then they'd have to give him a new one. This guy was giving me a headache.

We got everything hooked up and, of course, our listening line had the wrong number on it. I straightened everything out, got everything working and went back to Houston.

When I came into the office the next day, I saw Donnie, told him I was there and I was putting in for holiday pay for working on Monday.

"I'm not going to pay for it," he said.

"Donnie, it was a federal holiday. It's a law," I said back at him.

"I don't care, you can put in whatever you want on your time sheet, but I will not sign it," he said as he walked away. As time went by, he became more of a jerk than ever before.

Not long after that, it was time for our reviews.

"Come and see me for your review," Donnie said to me.

"Can we do it now?" I asked.

"I don't really have time, but I can squeeze you in," he said, trying to sound accommodating.

We went to his office and sat down.

"You do a really good job, but you don't talk to people enough," he said.

"What?"

"When people call you, you give them what they want, but you don't talk to them," he continued.

"Donnie, we are very busy, so I ask them what kind of deal they are doing and what information is needed," I said. "Do I need to ask them about the weather?"

"No. You just need to start talking to them more," he said without further elaboration.

"Okay."

"You should know that I'm hard on these reviews and don't believe in good reviews," he said, sharing his brilliant management techniques. "Even if you do outstanding work, you will not get an outstanding evaluation."

I just left his office shaking my head.

Another time I was randomly selected for a drug test, so I got a call from Donnie telling me I had to go for a drug test and then he hung up. So there I was, sitting at my desk saying to myself, "He can't be that stupid. He didn't give me a date, time or anything."

I was not allowed to call him back. So I had to drive to the Division office and ask him where I needed to report and at what time. This is important stuff, because if you fail to report at your time you could get severely disciplined, suspended for up to 30 days without pay or even fired.

One more Donnie story and then I'll move on.

I was at my desk when Donnie called me and said, "Dave, when you report tomorrow, internal affairs is going to be here they want to interview you."

Then, he hung up.

Holy Crap. What Could This Be About?

Now, I knew management was required to tell me why internal affairs wanted to speak with me and provide me with the time of the meeting. I quickly got on the phone with my FLEOA (Federal Law Enforcement Officers Association, which maintains lawyers for its members) lawyer, and told him I was supposed to meet with internal affairs.

"Your supervisor is supposed to tell you what this is about before any interview," he advised.

"I will call Donnie back and tell him what you said and then I'll call you right back," I told him, anticipating a real nightmare.

"I have just spoken to my lawyer and he tells me you are supposed to tell me the time of my meeting and the reason internal affairs wants to meet with me," I said.

"I don't know," Donnie said, "I'll let you know in the morning."

I called my lawyer back and he told me to just wait until I got Donnie's phone call and learn what they wanted. Because they were in violation of their own procedures, the meeting would be adjourned for 24 hours due to lack of notice.

With my lawyer's phone number in my pocket, I was called in the morning and told to be there at 10 o'clock. I notified my lawyer and he said, "Fine."

I went to the interview and told the internal affairs agents I did not know what this was about and that my lawyer would like to sit in on the conversation. The internal affairs agents were surprised by this, and said, "Whoa, whoa, wait a minute; this is not that serious of a matter."

It turned out that an administrative assistant in the office used official letterhead to discover the location of her ex-husband, who was still in the U.S. military, and she told internal affairs that I gave her the address for the source of that information. I admitted I gave her the address, which was public knowledge, but shared that I never told her to use official letterhead.

I also told them that on another occasion, when I was in New York, my trainer got in trouble and received a 90-day warning letter in his official file for sending his son a note with a recruiting pamphlet. He had done this because one of his friends was interested in becoming an ATF agent. I explained that I fully understood the consequences of misusing official letterhead for any personal business—even stamps.

The internal affairs agents were happy with my response and it was over in about five minutes. Then one of the agents asked me if I was at Waco. I told him I was, and he wanted to hear what happened. That conversation lasted almost an hour and a half. They were nice guys and we just had a talk about all of it and the time got away from us.

When I got out of the office, one of my colleagues grabbed me and said, "What happened?"

He was wondering why we were in there so long. I told him we talked about Waco.

"Oh! We all got nervous because you were in there for a while," he explained.

We had a good laugh. That was the only time I ever had to speak to internal affairs in my entire career.

Another Waco Squabble

In mid-May1994, the agents and staff who were at Waco were sent to the Xerox Document University in Virginia, to review the events of February 28, 1993. We were split into groups—by SRT teams, the agents from the U/C house, etc.

I had to choose between the U/C house and the SRT meeting. I talked to my TOO partner and he said he wanted to go to the SRT meeting. I told him I would go to the U/C house meeting, since at least one of us should be there.

The meeting had agents from ATF headquarters present, as well as all eight of the agents assigned to the U/C house. I wasn't one to keep book on anyone, or keep tabs on someone's activities, but from the onset I knew there was going to be trouble with this review.

The group discussion leader started out by asking, "What were the problems?" Of course the leader, Jeff (the agent who had the hat given to him by the owner of the ranch), spoke up and said, "The equipment didn't work."

I chimed in and asked, "What equipment?"

"The photo equipment," he said.

With that, I opened up my notebook and told them about my trip and how Steve Willis and I went to fix the camera problems. I also shared how we developed the pictures and reported back to everyone's satisfaction that the camera equipment did work.

I explained how we labeled and numbered each piece of equipment with instruction sheets and concluded by saying that, as of this date, I have yet to see any photos taken from the U/C house other than the ones I took.

He immediately quieted down. The next problem was brought up and I responded in the same manner, over and over again. I believe we did everything possible to make the U/C house work and I don't know if it was apathy, lack of ability, or not caring that kept it from effectively working.

The complaints didn't last very long; whenever they brought up a particular subject, I was quick to respond using my notes and calendar. I remember thinking, I'm not going to let either me or my partner take any of the blame for the failures in the U/C house.

Later that night at the bar we were talking to the then Acting ATF Director, Charlie Thompson. He told the agents to talk freely and do whatever we wanted as it related to Waco.

The following day there was an award ceremony, where they handed out medals for the first time in ATF history. The Houston division, I believe, only received one of them. It was presented to Dave, the agent who ran in front of me to get his fellow wounded agent.

SAC Donnie did not believe in awards or citations. He even commented to me, "Why should anybody get awards for doing their job?"

To me, it's not so much that you need recognition for your actions, but sometimes in a situation like this, it rewards the action you did take. A lot of comments were made after the awards ceremony about the lack of awards for the Houston division. Some agents in other divisions suggested we were being punished because this case originated out of our division.

The next day there was a memorial service at the National Law Enforcement Memorial in Washington, D.C. It was moving. The New York City Police Department Drum and Bagpipe Corps performed. Afterwards, there was a reception at a building just beyond the Memorial. Everyone attending was then invited to the local Fraternal Order of Police Lodge where we were able to meet the officers from New York City, and I caught up with some agents I hadn't seen in a while.

When the New York City Police Drum and Bagpipe Corps was leaving on the bus, one of the officers opened the rear roof emergency hatch, sat on the roof and started playing the bagpipes as the bus took off down the road. It was quite a sight.

On the last day we took the D.C. Metro to what is now called Reagan National Airport, for our flight back to Texas. Who was on that same Metro train? It was Don, my first supervisor in Texas, who had transferred to D.C.

"Are you working?" I asked him.

"No. I took the rest of the afternoon off," he said.

He then went on to say that when he showed up at ATF headquarters in the morning, he'd take a jacket from the back of the door and hang it on his chair. Then, he'd open a file, place it on his desk and leave for the day. He explained that he would return at lunchtime to check his messages while everybody else was out, and then leave again.

Unashamed, he concluded by sharing that at 5:30 p.m., he'd return, hang the jacket on the back of the door and close the file, placing it in his desk before heading home.

He was promoted to a GS 15 before he retired, and relocated to the Phoenix division as an ASAC, where he once again distinguished himself during the Columbine shooting incident. In the shooting's aftermath, when authorities were looking for any bomb techs to help search the school for IED's, he refused to send a nearby certified explosive specialist because he didn't like him. He ordered him to stand down and not respond to their request for help.

On History's Periphery

On Christmas Eve morning in 1994, I got a call from ATF headquarters and was told to put a RDNR on the telephone line they believed belonged to the Unabomber's mother. I was contacted later in the day with the warrant and given the location for hanging the equipment.

It was past five in the afternoon before I had all the information I needed, and it took me about an hour to get to the location. I opened the box and discovered it had been installed in 1945!

I started hanging the equipment and performing tests. I then hooked up with my phone butt set to another pair in the phone box and called headquarters to do a test on the equipment I just installed. The device malfunctioned, and I did not have access to another unit. The Tech in D.C. told me to hang the RDNR anyway and call him back in 30 minutes to learn what they wanted to do.

I called him back from the box, and was told the units should record any activity, but I had to download it manually at the site. That's what we did, and I ended up calling Judy from that box letting her know I would not get home until about nine o'clock. That was my only unique connection with the Unabomber case.

On April 19, 1995, the bombing in Oklahoma City happened. I was at a doctor's appointment sitting in the waiting area and watching the news. You could see the destruction from the news tape being shown, but they did not give a location. The "on the scene" reporter was saying to send everything—police, ambulance and fire—but never disclosed the incident's location.

I called my TOO partner and asked him, "Was anything going on in Houston?"

"No," he said.

"Are you watching the news?" I asked him.

Over the phone I could hear a phone ringing and then he said, "Oklahoma City."

I had a gut wrenching feeling. He told me he would call me if I had to come in after my appointment. The next day at work, the agents were told to stand by and be ready to travel.

The day after, we had SRT training, and on our way to training agents were being called on the radio and told to head straight towards Oklahoma City.

An agent who went there told me they were actually finding body parts up to three blocks away from the seat of the blast. He told me the TV did not do it justice.

I wasn't called to go to Oklahoma City, but there was a guy in Tyler, Texas, trying to buy explosives to blow up the IRS center there. I ended up putting up an RDNR for the case. It was a very stressful time, because you didn't know what would happen next, whether or not this was a lone wolf attack or the start of a bunch of attacks on the federal government.

You can never understand the devastation created at one of those scenes unless you've worked them. There are very few intact bodies recovered due to the grinding affect of the falling building. It's just nasty.

Later on, I did a 30-day detail as an operations officer. In that role, all the paperwork goes through you and you have to check it before it goes up the food chain to be signed. Talk about a mind-numbing job!

All you do all day is sit there and go through paperwork. It's a great teacher, because after you do that detail, you know everything about paperwork.

By now it was becoming increasingly clear to Judy and me that we didn't want to stay in Texas. It had a low cost of living, but Judy really wanted to be closer to her family in the northeast. So, I started putting in for jobs, and I talked to my counterparts at headquarters.

I decided to go up to D.C. for a role as a senior tactical operations officer in the headquarters division. I was looking forward to getting away from Donnie, but wouldn't you know it, we both transferred to headquarters on the very same day. If I had known one week earlier he was going to headquarters, I might have stayed in Houston for the rest of my career.

Chapter 7

WASHINGTON, D.C.

The View From the Top

In early February 1996, I transferred to ATF headquarters in Washington, D.C. Since I was working at the ATF lab, my office was in Rockville, Md. When Judy and I arrived in Maryland, we were greeted by one of the biggest snowstorms to hit the area in a long time. It was so bad I had to put my truck into four-wheel drive just to get into the parking spot.

Day one, you would think being transferred to headquarters would warrant at least a one-day orientation, or some kind of briefing regarding the job and its duties. That was not the case for ATF. I spent the rest of the day unpacking and familiarizing myself with my new surroundings.

When I got to my new position, I was told by my supervisor and peers I needed to hit the ground running. They were not kidding. One of my new responsibilities was to order all the vehicles for ATF. The agent who preceded me in that role told me it was not a big deal because ATF only averaged 60 to 70 new cars each year due to the limited budget. Still, you had to pick out everything from color, interior, engine size, mirrors and accessories. Then there was dealing with the General Services Administration! At first it didn't seem like a big deal.

Day two, my supervisor, Dick, who was a great guy, and who was one of the top supervisors of my career, took me to the D.C. headquarters. He showed me where the acquisition people were and with whom I'd be working. I also was introduced to our contracting officers.

I was brought up to what was then known as "the eighth floor." The eighth floor was where all the senior management offices were located. Due to the events in Waco, ATF was restructured with a full blessing from the Treasury Department. The restructure added yet another layer of management called DAD (Deputy Associate Director). The DADs were located on the eighth floor.

While there, I was introduced to a DAD whom I had met about one year earlier in Chicago.

"Dave, have a seat," he said just after Dick asked if he could use the restroom.

"Dave, you want to hear the secret in headquarters?"

"Sure," I replied, not really certain where this was going.

"The secret to headquarters is that nobody knows what they're doing," he said without the slightest change of expression.

My head was already spinning from all the people I met that day, and this was just another bump on the noggin. They were killing me. We talked for a little longer, and he wished me good luck at headquarters.

Dick and I finished our tour and I went home. That evening, I told Judy what happened and said, "I hope I can make it through this!" Then we shared a good laugh.

By the end of that first week, I was informed we had more than $12 million with which to buy vehicles and it was my sole responsibility to get the order done by the last week in February. It turns out that in the Waco aftermath, there was a push for additional funding to the agency, which led to an influx of cash. I had less than two weeks to spend it. Dick, my new boss, told me if I had any questions or problems to talk to him and not the previous agent in charge of vehicle purchasing. I am not sure exactly why, but I think Dick did not want me to be unduly influenced by my predecessor. I am sure he had his reasons!

I was thankful Judy had the skill sets she did, because Excel was relatively new and I had no experience whatsoever in working with it. She gave me a crash course that helped me tremendously in keeping everything straight on the more than 800 vehicles I was purchasing. I also had to manually retype and verify delivery points for each of our 24 divisions, as well as Alaska, Canada, Colombia, Hawaii, Puerto Rico and the Virgin Islands.

A few weeks later, all the Tactical Operations Branch (TOB) agents and project officers received a memo from Dick that included the full scope of our duties. In the memo, I learned that I was the program manager for vehicle acquisition; fleet manager/coordinator; mobile command post vehicle manager/maintenance coordinator; and responsible for surveillance video, electronic tracking, and the chemical taggants program. I also served as the warehouse manager. The warehouse was where ATF stored goods. It was a big place requiring me to learn to operate a forklift. In addition, I was the branch property custodian, Property Plus (an inventory control program in the process of being implemented by ATF) transition coordinator, and program manager for long-range surveillance for video and photography. I was also a COTR (Contracting Officer Technical Representative) for law enforcement vehicles, vehicle sirens, lights, alarms and basically anything else related to vehicles.

Obviously, it was a big job. Being a program manager—or a commodity manager—meant you were the material expert for that commodity, and responsible for the budget and implementation of the commodity.

The equipment commodities I was responsible for maintaining and on which I was to become a material expert included vehicles, vehicles acquisitions, photographic equipment, binoculars, and long-range lenses. I was also the military surplus equipment coordinator. The committees on which I represented ATF included the Treasury Department Fleet Manager's committee and the Treasury G-8 committee on computer crimes. The latter was an interesting committee, as the meetings were held in the old Treasury building—originally constructed in 1836 and rich with history.

If anyone in ATF had any question about any of these many items, no matter how big or small, they called me. It was an insane amount of responsibility, with a great deal of money to spend. I remember signing requisitions for well over $12 million, and wondering how long I would last in this job if I screwed up. Much of my concern was related to the fact that vehicles were a touchy subject across our agency.

A week or so later, I was unofficially told by someone in the Houston division that ATF was going to have another award ceremony to make up for the lack of recognition we received for our actions in Waco. I was also told not to travel back to Houston to receive my award. This kind of bummed me out. I figured they were going to send it to me in the mail, which was better than never receiving it at all, I suppose.

Later on, I learned through my boss that my award would be presented at a town hall meeting in D.C. Our new director, John Magaw, liked to have these town hall meetings from time to time. So on February 20, 1996, in the middle of all this craziness, I was told that I would receive an award for my duty in Waco—almost three years to the day since that action.

I took Judy to the ceremony. Director Magaw read a summary of my actions for that day, and I was credited for stopping the flanking movement of the Davidians, while under tremendous gunfire. After his comments the director said, "I do not know why it took so long for you to get this award, but congratulations."

After the awards ceremony, I sat through the town hall meeting with Judy. The head of each directorate attended. Magaw believed in a flatline management system. As you may well imagine, this is an ineffective system, especially in the government where everyone is made equal.

For example, the training department was on the same level as field operations, which covers ATF's primary responsibilities in the field. In this set up, training could dictate street policy. If the Army had the same management structure as ATF, the cooks could say, "No, we don't want to take that hill," because they have the same authority as the officers leading the troops. This system only worked in the business world if you had a strong leader, and that was certainly not the case for us.

The meeting was grinding on and on when an agent stood up and said, "My computer does not work."

The agent associate director in charge of the IT section stood up, and said, "Mine does not work either," and sat back down. Judy and I looked at each other, and did all we could to not burst out laughing. After the town hall meeting, we left the building. Judy commented on the unprofessionalism of our management staff. She couldn't imagine responding like that to any question during a meeting and getting away with it. I agreed and reiterated, "I hope we can survive our time here in D.C."

I ended up doing the vehicle orders from 1996 to 1999, with my biggest order coming in 1997. That year I ordered 805 new vehicles with a total purchase of $16 million.

Being in charge of the vehicle ordering was crazy. Everyone wanted a favor or an additional car, and if you did it for one you had to do it for all.

Everyone from SACs to the newly hired street agents called me, asking if I could get them a car other than the one they received. The craziest call was when an agent called me and said his wife told him the car's color didn't look good in the driveway! Here I was, dealing every day with all kinds of craziness, and this guy was complaining about the color of his car.

"You should turn your keys into your supervisor," I told him.

"When will I be getting the new car?" he asked.

"It depends on what kind of cars we order next year," I replied with a snarky tone.

He didn't fully understand what I was trying to tell him, so I said again, "Turn your keys into your boss and you can hope that next year's car order might have a color you want."

I guess he could tell by the sarcasm in my voice that what he was asking was simply ridiculous—but perhaps not the most ridiculous.

I had complaints about everything and compliments about everything. For example, I would get a call from someone complaining about a particular option on a car, and then an hour later another person would call me and compliment me on the same option in his car.

What was also crazy about the car orders was that the person in charge over at Treasury insisted we buy cars according to vehicle manufacturer market share in overall sales. For example, that meant you had to buy 20% Chrysler, 45% GM, and 35% Ford. Then on top of that, 20 percent of your total fleet purchase had to be economic vehicles, or subcompacts.

I also had to do special surveys by contacting every division to determine the need for vehicles such as Camaros and Mustangs for use as undercover cars. This was a contentious issue, because certain SACs did not want to count the undercover car against their vehicle allotment.

The way ATF operated, everybody wanted to leave his or her mark. We had an ASAC who was so egocentric, that when the new cars arrived he would pick out two or three that he liked the best, then have his operations officer stand in the parking lot while he drove by. He wanted to know what car he looked the best in.

After I created the spreadsheet for the car order, I told the approving supervisors that if a single item was changed the entire order needed to be changed, and we were under very tight time constraints. Even though the new fiscal year began in October, the vehicle purchase budgets were not received until mid-February, and the order had to be placed by the end of that month. We did it, but it was a relief to have the vehicle order completed due to all the politics involved.

The Olympic Centennial Games Go Awry

In the summer of 1996, I volunteered to be the TOO for the Olympic Games in Atlanta, Georgia. It was exciting. I was right in the middle of one the biggest happenings in the world, and had an ID badge allowing me access anywhere and into any event of my choosing. ATF was located at Dobbins Air Force base, which was also the bomb management center. The center was created to deal with any incident that may happen at any of the venues. I was directly involved in helping set up the command post. I was told the most important thing I could do was get cable television working in the center. With agents on duty all the time, there was plenty of down time and TV brought us relief from daily monotony.

The command post consisted of many little rooms that were divvyed up into little command centers. The main command center had one big room with rows of tables and chairs all facing forward.

Because we were located on an Air Force Base, we also had U.S. Customs helicopters stationed just outside the command center. It's amazing how many resources were in place to support this event. The public had no idea what was going on behind the scenes.

I worked the evening shift, and the local Atlanta TOO worked the day shift. The TOO wasn't very helpful. I would usually find him sitting in an obscure corner during his shift where he could not be easily seen.

I would check in at our command center, fix whatever problems they had, and then would join a roving assessment team. These teams were comprised of an ATF agent, FBI agent, a postal inspector and two Explosive Ordinance Disposal members from the U.S. Army.

The roving groups had particular venues to monitor and work. Our shift lasted from noon to midnight. ATF also had agents assigned permanently while an event was underway at a particular venue, and the agents had to stay at that venue for 12 hours a day for the entire 30-day assignment.

The events were all very exciting, with huge crowds. I find it hard to describe events like this. Seeing it on TV just doesn't do it justice.

The law enforcement officers also worked special events associated with the Olympic Games. We attended a dinner for the donors who contributed more than $50,000 (I was fortunate to stay for the whole event). To prepare for this huge dinner, there was limited time to sweep the building. I suggested we start with the entrances and then move on to the performers using K-9's and physical searches.

I was with the Army dog handler. We were searching the backstage area, when we came upon an actor's dressing room. The dog handler was a little hesitant about going in the room. I told him it was my call and if anybody was to bring anything in, it would likely come from someone just entering the area since all the buildings were swept several times.

With the limited amount of time available, it made sense to check out the areas with the highest threat. So, I knocked on the door and opened it. Inside there were maybe 15 people painting themselves with gold for their evening roles as living gold statues.

One of the actors told me they were getting dressed and asked if we could come back later.

"No. Everyone needs to stay where they are and not move because I am bringing a dog in to quickly go through the area," I said without hesitation.

I could see they were highly agitated and did not want to have any part of this.

"This is a requirement," I added. "We'll do a quick sweep of the room and then leave."

"I do not want to go in there," said the dog handler with a bewildered look on his face.

"This is why we do these areas first," I replied. "We don't have much time, and areas such as this have the highest likelihood of being an area where somebody would stash something."

"Nobody can deny us access to anything because national security trumps personal inconvenience," I added. "Besides, I'd rather have a complaint filed against me for doing my job than missing something that could have been prevented."

The search was finally completed. Nothing was found.

As the events progressed, all was going well, and we were settling into a routine, when, on July 27, the bombing occurred in Centennial Olympic Park. I remember getting off my shift, and going to the pool and having a drink. I was sitting with my feet in the pool water getting some relief from the day of walking. I then went to my room and fell asleep.

You know when you first go to sleep and you're in a deep comfortable sleep? Well, that was the state I was in when the phone rang. On the other end was one of the commanders at the command center. He was yelling loudly on the phone. I really couldn't understand what he was saying, so I finally asked him, "Where do you want me to be and how do you want me to dress?"

"Report to the command center and wear your blues," (referring to our blue BDU) was all he said.

Once I got to the command center, everybody was busy. There was a lot of commotion going on with agents gathering to learn about their assignments and identifying with certainty that an IED went off at the Olympic Games. We all knew what that meant and how it would affect the Games. Not that ATF had the final call, but we all wanted to be on the same page about what just happened. Everyone was checking and rechecking the facts. There was a lot of chatter.

After that incident, the whole mood of the Olympic Games changed. The device went off in a public area that had not required any screening. One of the assessment teams was notified that there was a suspicious object at the park, later identified as a backpack, and one of our ATF agents was dispatched to check it out. He saw wiring inside the bag, and immediately started pushing people away.

The backpack was leaning against the wall. It had a metal plate behind the explosives designed to direct the explosion in a certain direction. The bomber, Eric Rudolph, put a whole bunch of cement nails around his explosive device to inflict more damage with the shrapnel.

Fortunately, for all complexity of his explosive device, he had the IED tilted too far back and most of the debris went up into the air. Unfortunately, a woman was killed. She was in a position where the lowest piece of shrapnel struck her in the head.

I remember reading there were some people from her home town who learned she was the victim of the bombing, and they robbed her house the next day. It was pretty sad.

The following day was filled with briefings. The FBI had a briefing with all agencies involved, then told the non-FBI agents to leave the room and held a second briefing.

Before the Olympic Games started, there was a memo of understanding written for just this type of incident. If a bombing occurred, the evidence was supposed to be brought to the ATF lab in Atlanta for processing, with oversight provided by the FBI lab.

After this incident though, the FBI immediately threw out that agreement and wanted to take the evidence to their lab in D.C. They requested a Customs plane to transport the evidence from Atlanta to D.C. immediately.

The problem with that plan was the Customs flight team was from the D.C. area, and as with all pilots they could only remain on duty for a certain period of time due to regulations regarding pilot rest.

The FBI did not have all the evidence gathered in time for the Customs pilots to fly to D.C., so they ended up returning to their station and coming back the next day. This delayed the investigation process for another 24 hours.

This was about the time the FBI decided that their main subject was a man named Richard Jewell. He was a security guard in the area, and I believe he was the person who reported the suspicious package as well.

When ATF does investigations, it tries to get as much information as possible before the interview with the main target. This includes all the lab results, if possible. This did not happen. The FBI blamed Richard Jewell for the incident, and I heard a crazy story about their interview with him.

They knew Jewell wanted to become some type of law enforcement officer, so at the end of his interview they told him, "for training purposes," to act like he's confessing to the crime. When I heard this, I thought they were crazy.

He agreed to do it, and since the FBI wasn't getting anywhere, they threw him to the press. The press hounded him relentlessly because the FBI didn't do its job. Before the FBI interviewed him, they did find wire, wire cutters and other tools in his truck, but they failed to do a test on the tools, which could have been used to snip the wires recovered from the blast site. Personally, I think the FBI made a big mistake by not waiting for the lab work to be completed before conducting the interview, because later on it was determined that none of these materials had any connection to the explosive device.

Anyway, the evidence was sent to the FBI lab. When it arrived, they ended up calling the ATF lab in Rockville, Md., and had one of our technicians go the FBI lab in D.C. When the ATF technician saw the black powder used, he was immediately able to identify it. The FBI technician asked how he could identify it just by looking at it with his naked eye. The ATF technician shared that you can see the specks in the black powder that survived the explosion, but he assured them he'd run it through the spectrum analyzer when he returned to the ATF lab in Rockville, just to confirm.

The Games went into a security mode after this incident, resulting in everyone who came into any of the official Olympic Games areas being screened. Security also heavily patrolled all the other areas around the venues. This removed much of the festive air across the city.

The Games went on, but there was a lot of pressure to solve this bombing. I believe that, due to this pressure, many investigative techniques and protocols weren't followed properly.

Before the bombing, Customs had part of its air wing present to support the Games. They mainly used their helicopters to patrol over the Atlanta area to ensure any smaller planes entering the air space were chased off. A helicopter could fly above smaller planes and actually push them down with the propeller's downdraft. I thought that was interesting.

We were encouraged to take flights with them; it put more eyes in the air. I signed up with three other agents. It wasn't easy to get on a chopper, so when I learned that the pilot was into collecting Olympic Games commemorative pins, I gave him an ATF Olympic pin. I think this helped move me up in line!

One evening we took off for a flight. It was a typical patrol flight, and one of the agents sitting with me started to complain over the intercom about how there was no action during the flight. He jokingly began to question the pilot and copilot's manhood.

Suddenly a call came over the radio about a small plane entering restricted airspace. We were about 20 miles from the plane. The pilot quickly swung the chopper in the direction of the unidentified aircraft, dipped the chopper's nose down almost directly towards the ground and hit the throttle.

I was holding on and cursing the agent who had been kidding about their manhood. We headed in this direction for about two or three minutes before being told over the radio that the plane's pilot turned back. We then returned to a regular cruising speed.

After our patrol ended, one of the pilots told us we were heading back to the airport. Well, the agent who had earlier questioned their manhood started in on the pilot and copilot all over again.

That's when the pilot said, "Okay. We'll do the elevator."

I did not know what that meant, but it didn't sound good.

"We don't have to do the elevator," I pleaded over the radio as the other agents nodded in agreement.

The other agent would just not let up, so the pilot called air traffic control and told them they were going to do an accelerated vertical landing.

That still did not sound good to me.

As the chopper banked around I could see the air base. The pilot got on track for a runway, and as soon as he got over that runway, he immediately dropped the nose of the helicopter. It felt as though the helicopter was in a free fall. At just the last minute the pilot brought the nose up and gently landed on the ground. It was a speechless crowd that left the helicopter. The pilot chuckled, and told us all to come back soon. I was told later on that my experience was a rare opportunity. I guess I just didn't view it as much of a treat at the time.

It was a very exciting Olympic Games, but it was sad a woman died because of some idiot's delusion.

Approved by Dave DiBetta

It was a very busy time at TOB. Our agency was getting fully funded for the first time in a long time, and we were spending all kinds of money to upgrade and modernize our equipment. During my time in headquarters, I personally signed orders for well over $57 million.

I was probably traveling two to three weeks each month. I was all over the place. One of our main assignments in TOB was to help the field TOOs with more complicated investigations. For example, I'd get a call on Monday about an investigation with a technical problem. If it could not be resolved over the phone or by sending out a replacement piece of equipment, I'd be on a plane the next morning, arriving by afternoon to resolve the problem. The next day, I would recheck everything completed the day before then fly back home that afternoon.

When I flew, I was fortunate enough to hit every storm, whether it be thunder, snow, wind or hail regardless of where I was headed! It added to my anxiety about flying. Most of the time we flew out of Reagan National in D.C., and if you have ever flown in or out of that airport, you know it has a short runway surrounded by water. When the weather is bad, it is like landing on a Navy aircraft carrier. You're bouncing up and down over the river thermals and just as you hit the runway (varying because of the weather conditions), they slam on the brakes and you feel as though the plane just caught the cable on a carrier.

To say the least, it was a very busy time. I remember having at least two feet of paperwork on my desk and going through piles of stuff needing to be approved, reviewed, or requiring an action to be taken every day.

Another job I acquired was to approve the surplus vehicles—vehicles seized and put into government use. This was another touchy subject, because so many people were afraid of making a decision. They didn't want the responsibility that went along with it.

To help alleviate the perpetual question of "Who approved this?", I ended up getting a stamp that read, "Approved by Dave DiBetta." It was in big enough letters so there was no question who took responsibility for that decision. This simple solution prevented me from having to listen to administrative staff who would complain about doing things that might end their career. With my "stamp" of approval, I was responsible.

As warehouse manager, I called the ATF warehouse a monument to project officers of the past. The way headquarters worked, you transfer in, stay for two years, and then transfer out again. During those two years, an individual would be put in charge of a particular project. These projects would typically take six to seven months to figure out what was going on, what was needed, what was done before, and then it was time to wait until the budget cycle came around again. When an order could be placed, it would take time for it to come in and then it could finally be put it out for distribution.

This is why there's so much waste in government. By the time all this was completed, the agent would be ready to transfer out or would have already been transferred. I'd say that nine times out of ten, I was told to hold it for the next project officer. The problem was, when an agent left, it took about three months for the next project officer to arrive. There was no overlap or transfer of knowledge about the program.

As a result, the warehouse had a lot of dated and obsolete stuff that could not be sent out to the field. The medic program at one point purchased an entire pallet of more than 10,000 tongue depressors. Now, why anyone would buy so many tongue depressors I have no idea, but there they sat.

I was getting a good reputation for negotiating really great prices on all kinds of commodities. A number of the other agents would come up to me and ask how I got such great deals.

I would tell them, "It's simple. I ask the suppliers one question," and I could see their interest level peak, "I would ask them if what they quoted was their best price. The vast majority of the time they would take off another ten percent."

Many times it was as simple as that. But we would also do our homework. I was in charge of the photography program, and we were replacing the existing ATF cameras with the new Nikon 90 S. When you're purchasing well over one half million dollars in camera equipment, you want to make sure it is right.

I would ask my co-workers and the field TOO agents for their input. I would check the order with the manufacturer to ensure the equipment being purchased was compatible with gear already in the field or compatible with the new equipment that was purchased to replace the existing equipment. Unfortunately, not everyone considered this step a priority.

The different programs within ATF had different project managers. For example, one time the fire investigators wanted to buy new cameras for the field investigators. They came to me and asked for my advice. I discovered the flash they were purchasing would only work in the manual mode with the camera they were buying. This meant the sophisticated, highly automated "through the lens" option would not work due to a compatibility problem.

I shared this fact with the other project manager before he made his purchase.

"I want to use that flash anyway because I'm familiar with it and have used it successfully in the past," he said back to me.

"I think you're making a mistake," I said, and left it at that.

After the order was filled and equipment was sent out, I started to receive tons of phone calls complaining the equipment was not working. I told every caller to talk to the agent responsible for the purchase and bring it up with him.

I believe they ended up buying new flashes for the camera at great expense and waste to our agency. I hated to waste money on something that did not work and was not compatible with the rest of our systems. As a taxpayer, it bothered me to see such a misuse of government spending.

During my time in Washington, 1996-1999, we were conducting a lot of training at the Federal Law Enforcement Training Center, known as FLETC, in Glynco, Ga. The agency operated the ATF Academy at FLETC. Bill, the agent who transferred to headquarters with me, was about a year into this TOB assignment when he got in trouble for an alcohol incident on a plane.

At ATF, if you have any internal affairs action against you, you cannot teach at the Academy for two years. That meant that on top of everything else, more training instruction fell on me. I taught numerous classes including the Undercover School and Complex Investigation School, and served as a guest teacher for Advanced Video School and at Fort McClellan (where the SRT train) Covert Entry School.

During this period, ATF was rewriting the new agent-training curriculum. I rewrote the technical investigation part of the training, as well as the countermeasure section. I also helped revise the firearms section and helped rewrite the FLETC advance photography program.

I was also fortunate to attend many different courses while in TOB. One of the hardest classes was a two-month session called Fundamentals. It mainly dealt with countermeasures on electronic surveillance. A lot of State Department, CIA, Secret Service, Defense Intelligence Agency and FBI personnel were in attendance beside me.

In high school, your math teacher tells you one day you will use what she's teaching, and like every student who hears it, I said, "yeah right." This course was so complex, I used every bit of math training I had in my life and then some. The instructors all had field experience in countermeasures throughout the world, and some of the older instructors actually developed most of the equipment in use today. It was just a fascinating class, and I was lucky to be one of four ATF agents in attendance. I was really proud of the fact that I was one of the three ATF personnel who passed the course.

Heavy Loads and Wasted Money

Since I was in charge of all vehicle procurement, I was given the assignment of designing our new command-and-control vehicle, as well as to assist in the development of our new National Response Team (NRT) trucks, and the lab's new mobile laboratory. It was a good experience designing the command-and-control vehicle; I had total control over the project and that made it go much smoother.

When I was helping design the NRT trucks, I was working with another agent at headquarters. My boss told me not to take charge of the project, and to let the NRT program manager do that. That was fine by me, but the NRT people wanted me to work on the project because of the problems they were having with their program manager. It was clear the NRT program manager did not want to be in charge, but since it was her program, she was.

When we were given assignments, many times it wasn't because we had a background aligned to that assignment, but we were still expected to learn whatever task we were assigned to perform. I don't know if she was incapable of performing this assignment or had no interest in it, but they were having a lot of problems developing this vehicle. It got so bad for her that one night around nine o'clock the phone rang at home and unfortunately for me Judy answered. She said to me in a sarcastic voice, "There is a woman on the phone crying and she wants to talk to you."

This Doesn't Sound Good

It turns out it was the project officer, and she was upset about having to go test the vehicles she was purchasing. She was uncomfortable evaluating them without me being there. I told her she would do fine. It was an easy test, the vehicles were on a track and there was no open road on which she had to maneuver.

I went on to tell her I would be taking the design plans to the local fire company that had a retired Mack truck engineer on its team. I'd ask him to review our plans for any errors or something we may have missed. This seemed to calm her.

Within a week, I took the plans to this retired engineer for review. Some minor issues were resolved. One of the issues was the voltage requirement being at 15 amps. I learned most of the fire companies use 17-amp equipment, so we decided to bring up the voltage to 20 amps. It was little things like that. I had one more meeting with the project officer, and the project went off without a problem.

Another vehicle, even more complex to develop and with an incredible number of hands in the cookie jar, was the mobile lab. There were already problems in developing the mobile lab concept when they asked if I could help with the project. The company building the command and control vehicle was also building the mobile lab.

That there was going to be big trouble was clear, when the project team requested the requirements for the vehicle to pull this mobile lab trailer. ATF opted to purchase the vehicles before they developed the trailer. One of the members on the mobile lab committee told me directly that they didn't care about the trailer; they just wanted two Chevrolet Suburbans purchased.

"But you don't have the trailer designed and you don't know how much it will weigh," I tried explaining to them. "By buying the vehicles before the trailers, it will limit what you can design. That may limit your capabilities and that will be a mistake."

They didn't care. It was more important to them that they had vehicles they could use for other law enforcement activities—none of which were related to the mobile lab.

As sure as the day is long, the trailer design development was complicated by the limits on the vehicle's total weight and the many capabilities they insisted on packing into it. The towing capacity of the Suburban just wasn't sufficient. They ended up with a trailer that was very expensive and was at the Suburban's maximum towing capacity.

I also warned them that due to the severe weight of the trailer, it would be more difficult to pull, but it fell on deaf ears. The team ended up taking a trip to the trailer's manufacturer, and there was great friction among the committee. After the first night of the visit, we all went out to a restaurant, and then to the bar for a drink. I could see how fractured the groups were, because they all hung out according to their specialties.

I went to each of the groups and asked them for their bottom-line requirements. I told each of them, "Whatever you want to put in this trailer, we need to know the following: the weight, the size, ventilation and electrical requirements. We are dealing with sensitive scientific equipment. We need to know the types of protection the power sources need, any special storage and vibration requirements."

I was just amazed this project was this far along and none of this was done. I also explained to them how the trailers needed to be balanced.

"We cannot put all the equipment to one side just because it's convenient for you," I said, "You have to spread the weight around equally to avoid problems while driving."

It was a productive visit to the bar.

The next day, we met with the company's engineers and again talked over the issues. I suggested we let the company design the trailer based on the specifications we provided, including all the equipment. My thinking was to see what they came up with first, and then we could tweak it from there. This seemed to work well. The trailer was back on schedule and finally delivered.

I later received a call from the company, telling me ATF was withholding the trailer's final payment because one of the committee members refused to sign the payment voucher. I confirmed that the trailer had been signed for as completed, and the company representative asked if I would talk to the reluctant member of the committee.

I asked this committee member why was he refusing payment, and he shared that he did not like the trailer design.

"Did you sign off on the final design requirements the company sent you?" I asked him.

"Yes."

"Did you sign off on the vehicle when you accepted it?"

"Yes."

"Then you have to pay the bill because you agreed to the design and to the final delivery," I explained.

He got upset with me, and told me he didn't want the trailer the way it was built.

"We went through all the specs, all the requirements and everybody on the committee signed off, including you," I said, my patience thinning. "You cannot withhold payment at this point for a disagreement you had with other members of the committee. Besides, if you persist in your denial of payment, the interest penalty will come out of your budget."

Reluctantly, he signed the paper. It was just crazy how you had to deal with egos, power struggles and worst of all, emotions, when it came to big-ticket items.

On the trailer's first deployment, everyone in the lab was afraid to tow it. They ended up getting one of the techs from my shop to drive to the first response. While driving to the scene, the driver of the Suburban towing the trailer got into an accident while trying to avoid another vehicle. Due to the mobile lab's weight, both the Suburban and the trailer swerved violently and rolled. Luckily no one was hurt, but there was a brand-new suburban and a brand-new trailer completely totaled.

I received a call late in the evening and was told about the accident. I had to go to some small town in Virginia to make arrangements for the vehicle and trailer to be returned to our lab. What a waste of good money. ATF ended up buying a box truck instead of using the trailer. The cost of the whole project was doubled because, as one guy said, "I just want the Suburbans." It was very disheartening.

Designing anything for the field was always stressful and time-consuming. Most of the items ATF designed were to have long-term applications. Another example of wasted money and design was when our agency decided to design its own IED robot. The person responsible for designing it was also an end-user, an IED technician (we called them Bomb techs).

By the time I heard about this robot design, it was already deployed to the field. One day, I was driving the command and control vehicle to a press conference. The man who designed the robot was out in front of his vehicle with the robot.

I walked up to him and asked, "Are you aware of this robot's problems?"

"What problems?"

"Well, your robot isn't able to drive over a broom handle that may be left lying on the floor by the maintenance crew when a bomb threat was realized," I said.

"That's not true, my robot can do that," he replied a bit testily.

We were standing next to a curb and I asked him, "Can the robot climb a curb?"

"Yes it can," he said.

The robot he designed had smooth wheels, maybe three inches tall and four on each side. It also had sheet metal around its base that was bent down to accommodate the wheels. The robot was maybe 2 1/2 feet wide and built low to the ground.

The robot's inventor backed the machine up and started directing it toward a curb at a 45° angle. There was no way this robot was going to jump the curb. The first time he tried, he hit it pretty hard. The robot bounced off the curb and was still in the parking lot. He did this three more times before he was finally frustrated and picked it up and put in the grass.

Adding fuel to the fire I asked, "Does it work in the grass?"

He started to put it in forward and the wheels just spun. The robot was not moving. ATF wasted more than one half million dollars on three of these robots that had no practical use at all. For what we paid for the design, manufacturing and delivery of those robots, we could've bought two robots commonly used within the Explosive Ordnance Disposal community.

After the robot finished spinning its wheels in the grass, the tech just walked over, picked it up and put it back into the truck. That was the last time I saw any of those robots. I did, however, become aware of a fix for the smooth tires. The robot got nubby ones instead, but it still did not solve the problem of being able to go over debris and objects commonly found on the ground after a bomb threat evacuation.

I talked to this tech years later and asked him how his robots were doing. He looked at me and said, "What do you mean? I had nothing to do with it." I just laughed.

Making the Most of My Situation

Judy and I had a great time living in D.C. because of my position and ability to do favors for the Secret Service, Library of Congress and other federal agencies. As a result, we had access to some really fascinating tours. We went everywhere. We toured the Treasury building, the Library of Congress, the White House, the U.S. Capitol. It was great. My friends and family also enjoyed it—especially the Christmases in D.C. We were frequent guests at the candlelight White House Christmas tour.

I also had the opportunity to attend meetings in places like the Treasury building, the Treasury Annex, CIA headquarters and several other interesting buildings throughout D.C. One of the most memorable meetings I attended was with the G-8 Treasury Subcommittee on Computer Crimes. This particular meeting was held in the main Treasury building, and when I went to the meeting I drove up to the Secret Service guard, showed my credentials, told him where I had to go and he told me to park right in front of the building. Once I was at my parking spot, I put my ATF placard on the vehicle.

The meeting itself was interesting and it was a short-lived committee—we only met three times. I took an ATF computer forensic expert with us to this particular meeting for a discussion on determining how to search someone's computer without violating a nation's sovereignty. They were looking to establish procedures.

One of the committee members was from U.S. Customs, and wanted the authority to go into a country electronically, enter the computer and then leave.

"That's a great idea," I said, "but that country would want the right to do that to us here in the United States. I don't think we could stand for that."

I suggested, given the technology of that time, we set up treaties. If you wanted to search an individual's computer in another country, you could have an expert take a snapshot of everything on the drive and then go through that country's court process for obtaining a warrant for that information and retrieving the information.

My thinking was, whatever the U.S wanted to do to them, they'd want to do to us, making many suggestions impractical.

The guy from Customs looked at me and then replied, "I still want to do that anyway."

I felt like I was protecting these nation's sovereignty, but I was just thinking how other countries would perceive this invasion and how our country would also perceive it. It was very interesting. I don't know if a formal report was ever written, but it was interesting to go to meetings in such old buildings where so much history was made over the years.

When I came out after the meeting, I had a parking ticket on my car. I just laughed because it was the Secret Service who let me in, but a D.C. officer gave me the ticket. I later resolved that issue. I still have the ticket.

By 1998, I had been in headquarters for more than three years and had requested reassignment more than 25 times. I made the "best qualified" list each time, which means I had the qualifications for the job, but I was never selected for any positions.

My direct management changed, including the person who was the head of my directorate. She was being forced out of ATF because of an incident she had with a government car in Mexico. So I had no one in my corner to promote me.

I tried talking to Donnie, but all he told me was I did not have any management experience. I reminded him of all the management-acting positions I had under his watch while we were in Houston, and told him of my supervisory responsibilities and acting positions here in headquarters. He replied it wasn't enough.

So when I went back to my office, I told my boss what happened and asked if I could do more 30-day details when possible. A 30-day detail is when you act in a supervisory capacity in one of the many headquarters' programs. It was designed to provide agents with more supervisory experience. A few weeks later, the next detail was an acting chief position at the transnational branch in our intelligence division. Because of my security clearance status, I was selected for this assignment.

When I first showed up for this assignment, the supervisor was gone. I went to the secretary and asked for a phone list so I could identify the people I was supervising for the next 30 days. I reviewed the list and found I was in charge of one agent and four intelligence analysts.

I needed to attend a 7 a.m. briefing each morning and a 1 p.m. briefing after lunch. After the initial briefing on that first day, I spent the rest of the morning locating the people who were assigned to me. They were all on the same floor, but spread out.

One of them said to me, "You are the first supervisor I've seen in more than two months."

"Well, each morning after my briefing, I'll stop by each station to say hello and see what you're doing," I replied.

To my surprise, they seemed extremely excited about that. I guess it showed someone was interested in his or her job. The time went quickly and on my last day, the regular supervisor had returned from his assignment.

I was walking in the hallway past a small meeting he was conducting and can remember him saying, "If I was in charge, Waco would've never happened."

His name was Mark Chait. His statement stunned me. I think it's interesting that in 2012 he was made assistant director of field operations during Operation Fast and Furious, the gun walking operation where ATF was letting guns go to Mexico without any tracking.

I guess the next intelligence chief could make the same statement and claim that under his watch, Operation Fast and Furious would've never happened. The irony just kills me.

Back in my regular position, my new supervisor, Brad, wanted to start a covert entry team that could make entry via a warrant, enter the location, put in our surveillance equipment and leave undetected. I thought this to be viable. Over the years, I developed a few contacts with the CIA and they were under mandate to share techniques where possible to enhance law enforcement.

I finally set up a meeting between a CIA manager and Brad. I was asked to join him, and we got to the unmarked CIA building in Virginia and began laughing because all of a sudden, four plain-clothed officers started heading towards us. Just as they got within a car length of us, I told them we had a meeting inside.

They escorted us to the meeting room, where the gentleman we met with asked, "How can we help you?"

I shared with him where we were from and what our positions were.

"We're wondering if once you become comfortable with us, could we either take some training with the CIA or have an instructor teach us whatever information the CIA was able to release to us?" I asked.

"I'd need to run that request through my management," he said.

Then Brad said, "What I really want is to have a black bag team trained for operations."

The kicker was that Brad told the CIA representative ATF didn't want him to do this, but he wanted to do it anyway. The CIA agent just looked at me.

"Right now we just want to see what is available to us and how our agency can incorporate any information you can provide us," I said in a hurry.

Well, Brad again reiterated what he wanted to do and we ended the meeting.

When we were walking toward the car I said to him, "Why did you say you want to do something that your agency is against? They are not going to give us any assistance if they think you're working outside your agency parameters."

"That's what I want to do," he replied.

You can think it, but you should not have said it to them.

We never heard back from the CIA.

It was the end of 1998, and by this time it was clear I was not going to get out of headquarters via a promotion. The last straw was when I was acting supervisor for my branch and the evaluations came back. I noticed I had a lower evaluation than a guy who slept at the office in the afternoon and on whose cubicle you had to bang before you walked in to make sure he was awake.

I went to Brad, who was having his own problems, and he told me this is what his supervisor wanted. He told me that if he gave me an outstanding evaluation again, he would have to give me an award.

When you're in headquarters, everyone who does a good job gets an outstanding evaluation, which enables you to compete for promotion. So I asked to speak to his boss, Dale, and he said, "Sure."

The next day I walked into Dale's office and said, "Can I talk to you about my evaluation? I worked hard for the past three years and I'm trying to get out of headquarters."

"I don't like your writing," he said to me. "I'd rather have you sitting at your desk writing a memo that takes two weeks to complete and makes *you* look good, than doing all the work you do running around this branch to make *it* look good."

I was stunned. I asked him to repeat what he said and he did.

Then I think my rage just got the better of me and I said, "Screw it! Send me to Delaware."

"Dave, you don't understand. You are our 'go to' guy."

"Screw it. Send me to Delaware."

"Dave, any time we have a problem we send you."

"Screw it. Send me to Delaware."

My blood was boiling. That was the last straw. I just wanted to get out and I didn't care where, but I'm glad I said Delaware.

By the time the meeting was over, I must've said "Screw it, send me to Delaware" at least 15 times. When I left his office, I was told to wait outside and he called our branch chief. I got on the phone with her.

"Dave, are you certain you want to go to Delaware?" she asked me.

"I am," I said. "I put in for all these jobs, and I received no support for any promotions."

"Okay. I'll put in the request, but this won't be good for your career," she advised.

I thanked her and went back to my desk. I guess I was wasting my time working hard to support the field operation as opposed to working hard to promote my career, but either way, I was happy to go to Delaware.

Chapter 8

Delaware

Operation Kill Switch

In May 1999, I transferred from headquarters to the Delaware office, which was part of the Baltimore Field division. My supervisor, Stewart, was once an instructor of mine when I attended Special Response Team (SRT) School. I, in turn, had been his instructor in Complex Investigation School.

My first contact with him was on a Sunday night. He called me from his cell phone while driving at a high rate of speed in the car assigned to me. He was looking for an informant he'd lost in Virginia. He told me he would see me in the office the next day, and gave me the telephone number for an agent who would pick me up in the morning and take me to get my car.

When I arrived at the office, Stewart briefed me. He was working on a big motorcycle investigation dealing with the Pagan Motorcycle Club out of Pennsylvania. I also was told that this investigation encompassed white supremacists, the Aryan brotherhood and other motorcycle gangs. During the briefing on this I was thinking, *Holy crap!* I did not realize Delaware was the hotbed of white supremacists and motorcycle gangs in the U.S.

Just to give you my frame of mind at the time, I had just transferred out of headquarters after more than three years without a promotion. I had even applied for a job at HUD (Housing and Urban Development), because I had had enough of ATF's management style, and I was looking for a change. Unfortunately, I didn't get the job. I lost out to another ATF agent who was a firearms instructor, which was the job's primary requirement.

The position of TOO does not include casework. So, during my time in Houston as a TOO and my time at Headquarters as a senior TOO, a total of seven years, I did not do any casework. As a result, it was tough getting acclimated.

ATF management was always updating or changing the system standards for documentation. And as a result, I wasn't familiar with how things were done. And just to add to my frustration, it looked as though this big motorcycle gang investigation was being dumped into my lap!

I asked my supervisor, Stewart, if he would assign it to someone who had more experience working on this case. I went on to say that it had been a long time since I did investigative work and it would take me a little bit of time to get up on any new procedures. I still got the case—Operation Kill Switch.

On top of Operation Kill Switch, I was also informed that I was to become the training officer for Art, a new ATF agent. Art had been on the job for about a year. He had transferred into ATF from the internal affairs office at the State Department, where he was a special agent for ten years.

I was afraid of being overwhelmed, so at the risk of sounding like a broken record, I asked Stewart if someone else could at least take the training officer assignment as it was also something I hadn't done for seven years. I would later learn he had already asked two or three other agents in the office to be the training officer, and none of them wanted to take responsibility for Art.

Art would do a stupid thing just about every 30 days. It was just incredible! Just when you thought you had him in line, he would do something foolish again!

Within his first month with me for example, he was working with a local Wilmington detective in a high crime area of the city. Now, for the most part, Delaware has a low crime rate, but in certain areas of Wilmington, heroin use was an epidemic and firearms were always being recovered.

ATF vehicles had license plates from surrounding states and tinted windows—just like the drug dealers in the area. Art was driving in this area when a marked police unit pulled up behind him and turned on its lights. Art took off and a short police pursuit ensued. Art was traveling with a local detective who was urging him on.

Luckily for Art, nothing happened, but since Delaware has such a small police community, we immediately received a call in the office. Art's excuse was that the detective with him told him to do it.

"I don't care," I said looking at him in disbelief. "We are federal agents, and we do not mess with local law enforcement. It causes too much animosity, and personally, these local officers have enough stress on them. They don't need us messing with them."

Back to Operation Kill Switch. ATF brought in an undercover agent to see if he could infiltrate the local motorcycle gang. The operation had been underway for about six months at this point, and the only thing they had done so far was to get the Pagans' Sergeant of Arms to sell crack cocaine to an informant.

The undercover agent had only one objective: to get initiated into the motorcycle club and wear its colors. He would go out on Friday, Saturday and Sunday trying to get into the motorcycle club, but he was having little success. The only inroad he had made with the group was his undercover motorcycle kept breaking down and one of the local Pagans was helping him fix it. We were spending a lot of money on this investigation and getting nowhere.

It was clear to me the undercover agent had been on the case too long and frequently went off script with his story. One day, toward the end of the investigation, the agent was in our office when he received a call from a Pagans member. Instead of saying he was on the road, which was part of his cover story, he said he was at home. The Pagan on the phone said, "I'm just around the corner and I'll be there in two minutes."

After he hung up, I asked him, "Why did you tell him that? Why didn't you tell him you were at the store or on the road, which would have fit your undercover story?" The agent left the office and called the gang member back to arrange a meeting at another location.

In addition to all these other issues, the undercover agent had a Giglio issue. A Giglio is when an agent's record indicates that at some point, he or she had not been truthful during an official investigation. With this on your record, each time you testify in federal court, this information must be provided to the defense attorney. Having a Giglio would not end your career, but you had to be more careful in supporting everything you did or said.

The undercover also did not want to wear a wire or a recording device. He told me ATF only had transmitters that lasted an hour. I had a big argument with him, and had to show him several manuals to prove to him the minimum time for a transmitter was more than eight hours. I also had to explain to him that I was from the Tactical Operations Branch and I would surely know this fact to be true.

The investigation was basically being run by the undercover agent, which should never be done. The undercover agent had one goal, and we had another.

On one occasion he came back after a meeting at a bar, in which he, a target and the bartender, were hanging out. The bartender whipped out a white powder, and soon the bartender and target both snorted some lines of it.

The undercover didn't use any of the drugs, claiming he was on probation, which was his undercover story. After they all went home, we met with the agent and he said, "We got them now."

"Do you have any evidence?" I asked him, excited at the possibility of actually moving this case forward.

"No," he said, and so we called it a night.

The next day, I talked to him about the previous night's undercover meeting and asked him what he had.

"I have the target and the bartender using drugs," he said.

"Did you get that on tape?" I asked, knowing full well what his answer would be.

"No."

"Well, do you have any physical evidence then?"

"No."

Now, there are ways to get a drug sample without ingesting them, and it is a widely known undercover technique. Clearly, the undercover agent did not do it.

"How much undercover cash did you spend at the bar last night?"

"$60."

"Well, I don't think you have much. No recording of this drug usage at all, no sample taken of any drug, and you also spent $60 at a bar. I'm sure those two knuckleheads with you would say you spent the money on yourself. Plus, there are two witnesses against one; the three of you were the only ones in the bar!"

Once I got off the phone with him, I told Stewart about our conversation. I also reminded him the undercover had Giglio issues. In my opinion, the night was pretty much a waste of time. I was getting ticked. It was clear to me this investigation did not have a clear target, and the undercover agent was acting on his own, just trying to get the motorcycle gang's colors.

This investigation had been going on for nearly a year overall, and I was there for the last four months of it. During this time, the undercover was not completing any paperwork on this investigation. The required monthly reports were always late, as were the funding requests needed to run the investigation, which rarely were forwarded.

Unbeknownst to me, the delayed paperwork and other administrative issues were using up all the goodwill I had earned in headquarters. I later learned that my former colleagues at HQ were giving us a break by processing our late paperwork. I wish I had known this, because it certainly wasn't worth the cost.

Every weekend my partner and I would go and sit outside a bar without a break in the case. The undercover agent refused to record any of these outings. He resisted because I believe it would have shown what a waste of time this was and it would have become clear to everyone at ATF just exactly what he was doing.

The only excitement we had during this case was the night the undercover agent called my partner and I from his car just as the bar was closing. We were his cover team, and he told me he was hanging out with an older Pagan and the gang member's brother—who had just gotten out of jail. He said they were celebrating in the bar. He told us they were doing Angel Dust, and if you know anything about drugs, it's a very powerful hallucinogenic.

"They're looking to continue the party at their house," the undercover agent said.

"Hey, there are only two of us out here covering the deal, and if they are doing Angel Dust, they would kill you and not remember anything about your murder," I said in reply. "But, it's your call."

"I'm going with them to the house."

"What direction will you be going?" I asked him, already disturbed.

"I'm already two miles down the road," was his reply.

"In what f'ing direction?" I hollered back at him.

He told me and we started heading after him. I was with Agent Pat, and both he and I were stunned. We took off down the road at Mach 1, and I grabbed my partner's cell phone to call the supervisor and tell him what was going on.

We were racing down the road, when I received a call on my cell phone from the undercover agent. He decided not go to the house after all. While that was a wise decision in my opinion, this undercover agent had not used any tactics to keep himself safe as an undercover operative.

He used different doors as he left the bar, he never checked in, and there are specific ways of doing that without blowing your cover. After you go through a train wreck like Waco, as far as investigative techniques go, going through the same thing again was extremely frustrating.

I apologized to my wife, because many times I would just snap at her. One night, when I got home late, she asked me how it was going. I gave her a response like some kind of lunatic. Don't ask me why, I just had to scream. I'm very fortunate we are still together.

This investigation was going nowhere fast, and it was getting pretty hostile between the people in the office and the undercover agent. At one meeting, Stewart finally had enough. In the middle of a discussion, the undercover agent said, "The way you make it sound, it's my fault!"

"Yes, it is," Stewart said.

At this point, I think the undercover agent realized the end of this investigation was growing near. But there were more adventures ahead.

One day he called me and said he'd rented space in a warehouse by the Pennsylvania-Delaware border, to use as an undercover front. He realized that Delaware was a dry hole and the only way to see any action was to take the investigation to Philly. The problem was that Philadelphia was in another division, which required opening a new investigation. I doubt he would've found such an open environment as he did in Delaware.

We were wiring up the warehouse with cameras and other equipment, when the undercover agent informed us he was going to give the warehouse keys to one of the Pagan members. He had also decided to let the gang members store stuff in the warehouse lockers.

"This is crazy," I said to Stewart. "What if they murder someone and put the body in a locker in our warehouse? Does that make us an accessory to murder?"

I could tell by the expression on his face that Stewart was starting to realize that there were many bad ideas during the course of this investigation.

The straw that broke the camel's back occurred as we finished up work at the warehouse. The undercover agent decided to go to a motorcycle rally in Pennsylvania with two Delaware state troopers. They wanted to do this in an undercover capacity, so the three of them rode motorcycles to the event.

The undercover agent told me I was not needed, even though I was the case agent responsible for the entire investigation. So off they went. One of the state troopers, who hadn't ridden a motorcycle in more than 10 years, lost control, and nearly lost his leg. He was forced to go on a medical retirement.

That incident was something ATF management could not ignore. The Delaware state police wanted ATF to pay for his Worker's Compensation because he was acting as a task force member. The end came swiftly. I was told to immediately close this investigation.

I went to Improvised Explosive Device training the next week and the Baltimore ASAC, Jerry, came up to me and began apologizing for allowing this case to get so far out of control. Where had he been during the past four months? It was embarrassing that this was one of the largest investigations in his division, and this was the first time we'd spoken!

I later learned he was apologizing because he'd spoken with two other agents the week before and they explained to him what was going on with the investigation. I had been following the established chain of command, and incorrectly assumed my supervisor had been doing the same by keeping the ASAC informed of the investigation details and were operating with his consent. I spent the next several months trying to clean it up.

Stewart was transferred in December 2000. Before he left, he broke into the outer vault. To this day I don't know anyone who has any idea what he was looking for. After he left, we learned he didn't believe in signing any piece of paperwork at all. When he left the office, we literally sent a stack of paperwork four feet high to our division office. It had all been squirreled away in his office, hidden under his desk, under the dais, in his bookcase and all over the place.

ATF's management style was highly selective. They enforced rules when they wanted to. Allowing a situation such as this to happen was crazy. It's interesting to note that Stewart did get promoted two more times after 2000. Like we've all heard, "it doesn't matter what you know, it matters who you know."

That year was the first time in my career that I received a "fully satisfactory" rating on my review. I usually received an "outstanding" or "exceeds fully satisfactory." I guess after I threatened to write a memo about the investigative actions going on in this case, Stewart kind of lost his love for me. The entire operation was a complete disaster. There were unsigned evidence forms and an unreported $14,000 in the safe that was part of the investigation. I had to contact the prior case agent, who had been transferred, to have him come to the office and sign the incomplete property forms.

"I'm not signing it," the previous case agent said to me.

"Well, I cannot sign it, because I was not here when this evidence was taken into custody," I said back to him not hiding my impatience.

The agent finally agreed to sign the paperwork and when he finished, he threw down the pen and said, "This is bull crap!"

"Why? Because you had to sign for evidence you took into custody?" He just left the room.

Shortly thereafter, we got a new ASAC, Mike, a guy I knew from my time in headquarters. He told me he was disappointed in me and that he was officially closing the investigation. He wanted me to clean up the paperwork.

"We have a strong case on the Sergeant of Arms and we should at least pursue an arrest on that," I said. "That way we would at least get something out of this deal."

"I don't care," he said before the words had even finished coming out of my mouth. "Shut down the investigation."

I don't know what happened next, but I received a call a little later, and he told me to go ahead and prosecute the Sergeant of Arms. So that's what we did.

Because he was the Sergeant of Arms for the Pagans, the first time ATF did a search warrant on this guy the agents serving the warrant were required to use the SRT to search his house. However, when I was attempting the actual arrest, the Division Tactical Advisor, Brad, told me we did not need the SRT team. When I asked Brad what had changed, he couldn't give me an answer. I got the arrest warrant and arrested him without incident.

Since we didn't ultimately use the SRT, we didn't use the operation plan they developed, so I created one myself. It was the last one of my career. When Brad reviewed my plan, he told me to have Maryland State Police's helicopter land in a nearby field as backup in case we needed assistance. I was also instructed to have an ambulance standing by. Both of these requests were unnecessary, and an example of the over-the-top requirements he required to do a simple arrest, because he was new and had little field experience.

After we arrested the sergeant-at-arms, he jumped bail and was wandering around a development in Virginia when a sheriff's deputy drove past him. The fugitive literally jumped onto the hood of the sheriff's car and yelled, "The feds are looking for me! I've been on the run!"

At first they didn't believe him, and due to a glitch in the U.S. Marshal's reporting system, he wasn't listed as a fugitive until the day after he was arrested. That's when I got the call from the Marshals, telling me they had seized the three houses he put up for bond, as well as his vehicle. I just started laughing. The seizure of his assets probably hurt him more than the three years he got for dealing drugs.

My Trainee and Me

My trainee, Art, was getting increasingly hostile towards me. That was primarily due to the fact that much of the paperwork he submitted was being returned because of mistakes. Some of the paperwork was more than a year old, which led him to complain bitterly, "I thought this was done, how come it's only being returned now?"

Things became so tense I had to use a hostile-counseling technique I learned in college. In this technique, when you put the pen up the other party can talk without interruption, but when the pen is put down they have to be quiet.

This infuriated him even more, but as his training agent, I had to tell him what he was doing wrong in order to help him become a better agent. I had given him a lot of leeway, because he had 10 years as an agent with the State Department. But he had been an internal affairs agent, and that's a key difference. It is much easier to crack somebody when you are threatening him or her with security clearance than it is to crack someone on the street on whom you have nothing.

One of the most stupid things Art did occurred when we were out on an arrest warrant for a 24-year-old, 6' 4", 235 pound male, who just lost out on playing college football because of his grades. In other words, the guy was big.

We were being assisted by the Delaware State Police, who brought along their canine unit. We found out the subject was on the move and walking around his apartment complex. We learned he was headed toward the front of the complex.

Art and I were in my government car racing for the front of the complex. We tried to turn into a parking lot the suspect was cutting across, but two Delaware State Trooper units blocked it. They were busy talking. We swerved and went up over the curb, yelling at them to follow us. We did not have radio communications with them, since our radio systems were different.

At the start of the day, I had reminded Art to make sure he always had communications, and not to run too far ahead of the police officers. In a situation such as this, you did not want to be left on your own—especially with a suspect this size.

"If he slugs you and takes your gun, I'll shoot him!" I said to Art as the action heated up.

"Remember, there is a canine unit with us, and the dog picks up the first scent it finds, so don't get in front of the dog," I said to Art.

The dogs get excited and can't read, so if you are in front of the animal, they cannot tell what's on your police jacket and sometimes you could get a good bite.

As we passed the police officers, we saw the subject hopping over a fence. He recognized that we were on to him, and he quickly jumped back over the fence and headed back in the direction of the complex.

Suddenly, Art turned to me and said, "Screw this."

He got out of the car and began running toward the fence. By then, the dog handler was directly in front of Art. I watched as Art cut off the dog and began running into the woods.

The dog handler immediately followed him and I closed up behind the dog handler. We ran about a quarter of a mile into a clearing in the woods. That's where we found Art screaming at the top of his lungs, "Police get up! Police come out!" He said this over and over again.

I took off running towards him, and if you can imagine, we were in this opening with grass and weed cover about 6 to 8 inches tall. The subject was well over 6 feet tall, and Art was pointing his pistol at the ground telling this guy to get up—except there was nobody there.

"Shut the hell up," I hollered at Art.

"Did you see the suspect go into the woods?" I asked him.

"No," he said.

"Then why did you go into the woods?"

"I thought that is where he went," was all Art could come up with.

By this time, the rest of the officers were coming up behind us. I told Art to shut up and not say a word. I informed the arriving officers the target did not come in this direction and we all headed back to the apartment complex.

I tried to get a hold of the officer still waiting at the suspect's apartment, but I couldn't contact him. What I later learned was all the back-up came in our direction because the state police called in, but the target went back to his apartment. The other officers on our task force happened to be coming around the corner, literally ran into the suspect and arrested him on the spot.

I was furious with Art. He disregarded everything I said and left our vehicle with just a pager and no other means of communication. He ran ahead of all the other assisting officers without even looking back. I was getting tired of his stupidity and putting our operations at risk just because he wanted to be the hero who caught the bad guy.

Things just never seemed to get any better with him. On one of the last undercover operations I did with Art, we were trying to buy a gun at a local apartment complex. Art and I were part of the cover team, and monitoring the radio near the target area. Suddenly, over the radio we heard, "Are you trying to rob me? Put the gun down!"

The first rule in an undercover operation is not to rush in like gang-busters and put the undercover agent's life in danger. I was driving, so I started creeping up getting closer to the spot where the deal was going down.

The next thing we heard was the undercover agent struggling with the man who had the gun. The case agent got on the radio and ordered us to move in.

I gunned the car, raced around a turn, jumped a 12-inch curb, and exited the vehicle. They already had the one subject in custody, while another one took off on foot. Someone yelled out to go after him, so I ran toward him and another agent got in front of him and the subject gave up.

I quickly had him on the ground with my gun under his chin and told him, "Do not move or I'll shoot!"

I flipped him over and put handcuffs on him, and as I stood up the other subject's mother opened her apartment door. She heard her son screaming, "They got me and they're beating me!"

No one was beating him; they were just wrestling him to the ground. His mother opened her door, which was right in front of me, and released her pit bull on me. She was yelling, "Get him! Get him!"

I saw the dog coming at a full gallop from my right side. I turned and thought for a second about shooting him, but figured that'd be too much paperwork. So, as he ran towards me, I kicked him square in the chest like a field-goal kicker. The dog let out a loud yelp, and fell on his side about four feet from where I kicked him. He was whimpering, and quickly ran back into the apartment. We charged the mother with assault on a police officer and the dog had to be put down. That was sad.

We made it back to the police station and were finishing up. I sent Art to ask the case agent if there was anything else we needed to do. She asked him if we had any statements from the subject who had the gun and Art told her he would check.

He came back down to us as a group and asked if anybody interviewed the main subject. We had not and told him, "No."

The officers and agents involved were all busy writing notes. Unbeknownst to us, Art went to talk to the main target. After some time, Art came out of the prisoner's cell and said the person who was trying to sell us guns had given him a complete statement. I reminded Art he should have had a witness with him while he talked to the subject, but I told him to write up his statement anyway.

The next day we were in the office finalizing our paperwork, when Art brought in his statement from the primary subject. We reviewed his statement, and told him to include a description of when he read him his rights.

"I didn't read him his rights," Art said.

"Why not?"

"There were other more senior officers around that should have read him his rights," he said.

"Well, the statement you got from him is useless," I said back to him. "Do you understand what a custodial interview is?"

"Yes."

"You were conducting a custodial interview, why didn't you read him his rights?"

"It was the subject who began asking me questions," was his incredible reply. "I wasn't formally interviewing the suspect."

"Where was the subject seated?" I asked.

"In a holding cell."

"Was he handcuffed to the bench?"

"Yes, he was."

"He was in custody, right?" I queried.

"Yes."

"Well, what happened next?" I knew the answer and just waited for him to say it.

"I walked up to him and he asked me a question," Art said, "so then I asked him one."

"Did you then ask him any other questions?"

"Yes."

"In law enforcement, we call that a custodial interview. You blew it," I said frankly.

Art had been so eager to get an interview by himself, he jeopardized the entire investigation. Luckily for us, we had enough on these guys to take them to court. But, there's no excuse for losing the primary subject's statement.

This Can't Be Happening Again

Shortly after this episode, a position came open for the Diverse Career Impact Program (DCIP). It was also commonly known as the "division recruiter." I took the position because of all the craziness I'd been through in my short time in Delaware. I wasn't sure it would ever end!

DCIP was a good job, but there was one major problem, Donnie was one of my supervisors again!

ATF was undergoing a massive hiring push, and they were looking to recruit as many minorities as possible. Donnie had the bright idea of having HQ send out 50 employment packets to each DCIP agent (Division recruiter), which we were to mail only to minority candidates.

The non-minority applicants had to go to the website to download the documents and then submit them. Since Donnie was in charge of the hiring program, he adopted a first come, first served approach.

A TEA (Treasury Enforcement Agent) exam was coming up, with only 1,200 seats available for applicants. Overall, 4,200 people applied for those 1,200 seats. And because we had to mail packets to the minority applicants, their submissions naturally took longer to come back to us—usually by at least a day. None of the 50 applicants to whom I had sent a package made the test's cut-off date. At one point, I tried to talk to Donnie about not sending the packets out and having the minority candidates complete the information online like the others, but that wasn't the way Donnie wanted to do it. I swear the man had no concept of anything. I know we lost a lot of good applicants because of this process.

When I first got the DCIP position, I was sent on a 30-day detail in West Virginia. They were in the process of ramping up the mandatory background checks for purchasing firearms and the ATF team there needed support.

While I was away on this detail, things continued to happen. First, I had to write a recruiting memo for the DCIP program. A woman we were working with on the project had been the lead editor for the Defense Department in her previous job. She transferred over to ATF because it was less of a commute for her. I asked her to proofread the memo, and then submitted it to our Division for their review and forwarding. After a week, I asked them how it was. They said they fixed all the errors and sent it forward. I shared this with the woman. She said, "Your Division is crazy."

I wasn't teaching anymore since I left headquarters, and was no longer in charge of those programs. But here's another example of how ATF operates: While on my detail in West Virginia, they sent me to a one-week master instructor class so I could become a better teacher within the ATF. After I took that class, I never taught in the ATF Academy again! Nor did any of my classmates! What a great waste of money to have more than 40 people come from all over the country to attend the training class and none of us ever taught another ATF course again.

It Just Made Me Laugh

Back at the office, our acting supervisor, Dan, had come to Delaware on a temporary assignment from our training academy to cover Stewart's job after he had transferred. Dan wanted to shut down all investigations in our office in an effort to prepare for an up and coming office review. Art had been given an assignment to check on, and, if possible, retrieve a firearm part that had been sent out improperly. But Dan's directive meant Art's assignment had to be completed within a week. I was getting ready to leave for West Virginia, and he asked me what he should do.

"Ask Dan what he wants you to do," I said. "If he wants you to do the assignment, do it. If he doesn't, then it's on him."

Of course, Art didn't do that and decided on his own to not complete the assignment. It turns out, the assignment needed to be done, and as a result everyone in the office had to help him complete the work in one day. They all complained to me they had to cancel their duties for the day to help him get his work done. It was an angry bunch.

When I completed my monthly review for him, it had to be done over the telephone because I was still working in West Virginia. Art was highly upset, because I had written him up for not following instructions, which resulted in a poor working relationship with everyone in the office.

"Everything was going great since you weren't here, but now you are stressing me out, you are stressing me out," Art said over the phone. He was really agitated, and I couldn't get a word in edgewise, so I asked to speak to Bill, the new supervisor who had just arrived from headquarters.

Once we were off the phone, Art freaked out. The agents who wrote a report on the "incident," shared the statement of events that detailed the situation. He went into the evidence vault and started throwing things around. He then went back to his office, took his handgun and threw it into a filing cabinet. He began swearing and screaming out threats against me. People in the office were becoming concerned they would have to tackle him in order to subdue him.

My detail ended one week later. I returned to the office and told Bill I had to read the statements to see if I wanted to write a memo on this or not. ATF had a long history of agent-on-agent killings and assaults, and our manual order made it clear that if anyone threatened anyone with physical violence, it was supposed to be reported immediately to internal affairs. I got back on a Friday, and literally had a foot of paper work waiting for me, as well as the memo I had decided to write about Art's actions.

I sent the memo up the chain of command, and was called into ASAC Mike's office. As I walked into his office, I could see he had the memo in his hand.

"What's this all about?" he demanded as he threw the memo at me.

He's lucky it did not hit me, because I would have pressed charges for assault if it had.

"What's this all about?" he repeated.

"Did you read the memo? It's all in there," I said unsure of what was happening.

"Yes," he said, "and I took care of the matter by transferring Art out of your office."

"Are you sending my memo to internal affairs?" I asked.

"No, the transfer will take care of it," he replied.

"Well, is there anything else?" I asked.

"No."

"Thank you," I said as I left his office.

A week later, Mike, sent me a formal memo indicating it was up to me to decide if this incident was to be reported to internal affairs. I did not choose to pursue it. I was just glad to see Art go—and I'm convinced the rest of the office was as well.

Through all my difficulties with Art, it amazed me that no one in ATF management ever asked me what problems I was having with him or he was having with me, yet it was obvious to everyone else around.

I was enjoying the DCIP job, because it freed me from the Division politics, and I was able to do whatever needed to be done for this program. I was always at the top in the number of recruiting contacts as well as meeting any of the ATF's recruitment requirements.

Then 9/11 Happened

Everyone remembers where he or she was that day. I was in the office doing some paperwork and making phone calls. I had an 11 a.m. appointment at a local university. One of the agents came in and said, "Did you hear what's going on in New York?"

Someone said, "No."

He told us a plane hit one of the twin towers and they were sending rescue crews to the scene. One of the other agents went to another office where there was a TV. He called us, and provided an update on what was going on. By then, the second plane hit.

We were all stunned. I could feel the pit of my stomach just drop. No one officially knew what was going on, so I still went to my appointment. When I got to the campus, they were all watching TV news coverage. I watched with them for a few more minutes, and then told them I had to go and headed back to the office.

I was at the office when we heard the report of another plane with which air traffic controllers no longer had contact. That plane hit the

Pentagon. Everyone was getting highly agitated. We were listening to all of this on the radio, and then the phone calls started pouring in.

Most of them were just people we knew, asking us what was going on and if we had any more information than they did. My mother even got through and I talked to her. I told her they were going out for big buildings and if she went home she should be safe.

We were all in a group at the office, and I suggested we pick out a long gun based on seniority. Then, I said I was going to the bank to withdraw some cash in case something happened with the banks. I knew we'd soon be traveling, so I picked out an AR-15 rifle, then ran to the bank and grabbed $500.

Within an hour, two of our agents on the National Response Team (NRT) had orders to go to D.C., so they left to pack their gear. I was told to go to Baltimore to pick up one of the NRT trucks and drive it to D.C. We were instructed to pack for a long time away from home. One of our agents went to the Delaware Emergency Management Center. While there, he overheard the governor of Delaware ask on a conference call with all of the governors in United States, "Where is the President now?" A member of the Joint Chiefs of Staff inquired about who was asking the question. The Delaware governor responded, "the governor of Delaware." He responded, "Ma'am, you don't need to know that."

When I arrived in Baltimore, I reported in and was told to stand by; they did not want to move any additional assets in case there were counter attacks or secondary actions that required a response. I checked into a local hotel and watched TV; then checked in with my buddies.

I sat in Baltimore for two days, then it was decided to have me, along with the rest of the ATF agents in the area guard the entrances to the federal building in Baltimore. What a waste of manpower. Our upper management couldn't think of anything better for us to do, than to guard the entrance to a federal building?

It wasn't even a tall building. I thought we should be out there beating the bushes; finding out if there were any more plots, or copycat plots in the works in our area. To be honest with you, no one knew what was going on for the first couple of days. This kind of ticked me off.

There was one agent who decided to load up on weapons. He armed himself with just about every gun ATF had in its arsenal, and was standing next to me like he was going to stop a plane. I was finally sent home after a week and then placed on the local terrorism task force. I went to the first meeting, and during lunch I was asked if I wanted to be an air marshal. I told them, "No. I hate to fly."

Of course, I ended up being selected for this detail for two reasons. One, I was one of the better shots in the division. Second, I had no kids. The last comment really made me mad, because not having children had never brought me any advantage at any point of my career.

I was told to go home and pack. In the orders, it said we would be gone for one and a half years; that we were temporarily assigned to this program and had no other agency-related duties. The training was in Fort Dix, New Jersey, and it was to last for three days—that's how long it took them to process our IDs.

On the first day, we went right into training once the formalities of paperwork were completed. The Air Marshals training us shared that the most important thing was to protect the cockpit at all cost, and then explained how the cockpit doors on all the planes were being reinforced. One instructor said, "If you want to have dinner with the President, stop a terror incident in the sky."

The next day they took us to the range. They only wanted 90 percent qualifiers. They sent everyone else home. The range instructors were the Special Response Team from the State Department. They were all the same size and all had mustaches. After the first round, if you qualified, they set you aside. If you didn't qualify, you shot again. They gave you three attempts to qualify.

The guy who scored my target said I just made it; I was kind of surprised by that, because I did not get any shots outside the 10 ring. I was to learn later through my air marshal partner how they scored the targets. If they could see the bullet hole, they counted the hole. If you shot though a preexisting hole, you did not get credit for that shot. My partner was so good he failed the first three qualifications. When he asked the instructors how he could have failed since all of his shots were grouped within the size of a quarter, he was told how the targets were scored. They agreed to give him one more try. So, he shot around the entire 10 ring, with every bullet having its own spot within the ring. He finally passed.

After we qualified, they gave us 1,000 rounds of ammunition to shoot from the seven-yard line. We shot until all the ammo was exhausted. An agent from the State Department was trying to help us become better shots, but it just annoyed most of us. A female agent, who drove with me to the training, had previously served as a U.S. Marshal and was a good shot. The State Department guy was busting her chops about speed loading. She was telling him to leave her alone, and then he started yelling at her. I could see she was getting ticked, but she wasn't the type of person to scream at him.

Finally, I said, "Dude, leave her the hell alone." He turned and looked at me and I yelled again. Then he just walked away. She later told me she was just about to go off on him. I told her I didn't want her to get into trouble. Losing a team member would mean being on this detail even longer. We both laughed.

Going Airborne

It was pretty interesting flying as an Air Marshal. We got on the planes before the passengers and joined the crew in searching the plane. We then gave the crew a briefing. One of the first flights I took to D.C., you could clearly see the devastation wrought on the Pentagon. At first I flew from Philly to Dallas, then they moved me to Philly to D.C.—four flights a day. During the Salt Lake City Olympic Winter Games, I flew from Philly to Salt Lake City, then to Pocatello, Idaho, with a return trip the next day.

The first time I flew into Pocatello, I looked out the window and could see a small building with some lights sticking out of the snow. We landed on that snow after circling the field couple of times. When we were landing, I was thinking, They've got to be kidding! We just flew over the mountains, with the upper drafts.

That was quite a fun trip. Here we were landing on the snow and to keep us from sliding off the runway, the pilots had to use the engines to keep the plane aligned by revving one then the other. It was crazy.

The next day we took off in a blizzard, but the ground crew failed to remove the intake cover on one of the turbo props. As the pilot was starting the engine, I yelled, "The cover's on! The cover's on!" The pilot was extremely thankful the cover didn't get sucked into the engine. He thanked me profusely. I would have asked them for my money back for the flight, but I was already flying for free!

When we first began flying out of D.C., there was no one on the planes at all. On an empty flight, flying out of Reagan National, the pilots decided to fly with the cockpit door open so they could talk to us during the flight. One of the pilots asked if my partner and I wanted to do an elevated takeoff.

"No!" I hollered.

But my partner said, "Yes."

The pilot called into the tower to inform them the plane was using an elevated takeoff technique. We raced down the runway and as soon as the wheels got off the ground, it felt like we were going straight up. I thought I was going to break the seat—I was holding on so tightly. After the flight, I was going to shoot my partner over this issue.

We were paired with a partner for only two months and then rotated. My first partner recorded the mileage we flew those first two months, and it showed we flew around the world twice. During the 2001 Olympics, my new partner and I were headed to Tulsa, Oklahoma. We flew a couple of times from Tulsa to Salt Lake City, and then just sat in Tulsa for a couple weeks since they suspended our flights into Salt Lake City. I don't know why.

After this brief detail, we went back to flying D.C. to Philly routes. One night, I got a call at 11 o'clock at night telling me to get out of my Philly hotel and drive to D.C. I was instructed to call in when I got to our hotel. I got to D.C., checked into the hotel and called the control center. They told me I had a seven o'clock flight to New York that morning. It was already 3 a.m.

That day I got to see the Pentagon being repaired and the cleanup effort at the World Trade Center. When I first started flying that route, I could still see smoke coming up from the area where the towers went down. As a New Yorker, you kind of know the skyline of the city. It was so weird not seeing the towers anymore and discovering just how damaged that whole area was. It was very sad.

The detail ended as quickly as it started. I never knew when I would finish my time as an AM. Lucky for all of us, it was only a six-month detail. Hats off to my friends in the Air Marshal Service.

We learned our old director, Magaw, was asked to take over the new Transportation Security Agency (TSA). At one of his confirmation hearings he indicated he didn't want to talk about what he was doing to improve the screening process at the airports; he only wanted to talk about what the TSA patch meant. He later resigned due to health reasons, but it was clear the writing was on the wall—TSA was going to kick him out if he did not leave.

More Adventures in Delaware

It was late May or early June 2002, and it was good to be home, sleep in your own bed, and be around family for the summer holidays instead of flying on planes. A month or so later, our Division was having an awards ceremony. The other AM and I were getting awards for our service.

The new SAC was our former ASAC, Mike. He showed his dislike for me when it came time to present the awards. He began the ceremony by sharing how the first agent worked long hours, flew all the time and worked over holidays. He went on and on about how tough it was for her. In reality, she was very fortunate. She flew out of an airport that was about 20 minutes from her home and slept in her bed every night for the entire time she was on this detail.

When it came time to present me with my award, he looked down at it and said, "Oh yeah, Dave was there, too."

What a jerk. Even if he didn't like me, he still could've said something as simple as, "Good job." But he had to say that. Until the day I retired, my fellow agents would bust on me by saying, "Oh yeah, Dave was there, too" whenever they were discussing work-related items. I laughed every time I heard it, but I thought it showed how unprofessional ATF management was for the SAC to have ever said it in the first place.

A little while later I was assigned another trainee. His name was Sam, and at least he had real police experience. Around the same time I started getting ATF involved in the NASCAR races at Dover Downs. Sam and I were getting involved with everything from employee training to IED sweeps of the racetrack and grandstands.

I worked the races for about six years, and based on ATF's budget, if they had the money they would pay overtime and other times we would just work through the weekend without pay. The agency had certified explosives specialists that ATF management wanted at these events, but these agents would only work if they were going to be paid overtime. It was disconcerting that certain agents could refuse assignments based on pay without experiencing any repercussions. ATF was always good at selective management. All in all, working the races was exciting, and in 2008 Dover Downs was selected as the safest track in the country. I was very proud of us as a group.

In October 2002, the D.C. sniper first struck. It was unnerving to be in areas where at any second you could be shot dead just because you were there. As usual, the FBI profilers said it was an antisocial white male in his 30s, which made him a loner. I mean, come on. If you look at any profile done on any investigation where there was no clue as to identity of the suspect, 99.9 percent of the time the FBI profilers claim it's a "white male in his 30s, antisocial, loner." In this case it was a shame. I think if they had just let the police and investigators do their job, they may have caught those guys sooner.

During the investigation, a letter was found at one of the scenes and the investigators were not sure how to open it without contaminating it. Simply putting the letter into a large bag, slicing it open and keeping all the contents secured within the bag could easily have resolved this issue. The letter could have easily been removed from the envelope while still in the bag and once the letter was read and photographed, then the bag sealed and sent to the lab. By the time the letter was processed, another victim had been shot.

I think sometimes on these bigger investigations that the people in charge have a fear of making a decision because that decision could possibly jeopardize the investigation. Sure, sometimes it's a tough call, but that is why they get paid the big bucks!

At a press conference during the investigation, our ASAC, the one who decided to have us guard the federal building in Baltimore, mentioned how cowardly the sniper was. I believe he even went so far as to question the shooter's manhood. I'm not really sure of the purpose behind his words.

The Division committed to having the NRT truck at a Maryland Police show, so that weekend I had to go into the D.C. sniper area to deliver the truck. This is great, our boss just questioned the sniper's manhood, and now I'm headed to an open field with a huge ATF truck while wearing an ATF T-shirt.

I was with a younger agent and he said, "If I knew he said that, I would not have come out with you today!" I just started laughing. Anyhow, our NRT truck won best in category. It was the very truck I worked on during my assignment in Headquarters!

In 2002, ATF started a program requiring mandatory physicals each year. For some reason, ATF would not give me one. I had just been asked to join the National Response Team (NRT) by the northeast team leader. I was asked for a number of reasons—my skills as a photographer, my experience as a TOO, the Olympic Games, my years at headquarters and my involvement with NRTs over the years.

These teams specialized in arson and explosives investigations. Comprised of senior agents, NRTs would kick start an investigation and turn their findings over to state investigators or to an ATF agent working with the state police.

It seemed management was looking to deny my application for any reason. First, there were too many NRT members in our group. In fact, there were two. Both of those members agreed to resign from the NRT when they first heard about the problem. But Joe, the ASAC, did not want that to happen.

I don't know if this had any impact on management's decision or not, but I had just become the Federal Law Enforcement Officers Association (FLEOA) president for ATF. In federal law enforcement, we were not permitted to unionize, but we were allowed to have associations. In this role, I represented all ATF agents throughout the country. I figured taking this position was the kiss of death for my career. ATF management had a problem with whoever the representative was; in this position you were the one responsible for bringing up issues that were not favorable to the agency. As a result of management's failure to allow me to get a mandatory physical, I decided to file an EEO complaint that took six years to resolve. A colleague told me when I filed my complaint that it was a waste of time and I'd have to spend years on the case. They were right, but it was something I believed I had to do.

It was interesting that after I filed my EEO, I was asked a second time by the northeast team leader to join the NRT. Again I was denied. I had to file a retaliation complaint, which took four years to settle. I also filed a grievance on a separate matter with ATF that took only five years to resolve. It was a shame that ATF management took so long to settle these issues. I believe each issue was justified. It's disappointing that reaching a resolution to these situations took more than a fourth of my career. I ended up settling all complaints, and a year before I retired, ATF management finally allowed me to join the NRT.

As FLEOA president, I met annually with ATF's directors. Some directors refused to meet with me. Due to my experience dealing with my own EEO issues, I had some insight as to how agents' problems should be handled. Now I had the venue to share these insights and to shed light on their complaints. I was proud to serve as our agency president. It was a good feeling to be able to tell an agent where he or she could get help and to bring their issues to the attention of ATF management. In the best cases, we were able to help employees do their jobs better.

Athens, Another Olympic Games

In the summer of 2004, I was selected to go to the Olympic Games, in Athens, Greece. It was explained to all the officers on the assignment that due to the country's proximity to the Middle East, being attacked was the primay concern. The U.S. sent FBI agents to train the Greek police on driving techniques and general police tactics. Twenty-five ATF agents were sent to augment the Greek police in protecting the athletes as they were transported to their venues. The U.S. paid a substantial share of money to provide security during the Games.

The Greeks had different rules of engagement policies than we did. In the United States, if someone pointed a gun at me, I would be justified in shooting him or her. In Greece, you actually had to be shot at before an officer could shoot. The Greek officers also carried balsa wood clubs, and ball round ammunition, while we carried metal asps, and Hydra-Shok Jacketed Hollow Point rounds.

The U.S. Government flew us to Greece in an unmarked plane. It was a great trip, and I remember flying at a very high-altitude and seeing several thunderstorms over the ocean as we approached Europe. We received all kinds of credentials and paperwork in order to carry guns in Greece so we could do our job.

It's interesting how you automatically bond with other Americans when you're overseas. I found this to be especially true during the Olympic Games. There's great pride in your country, and everyone is happy to see their country's athletes do well.

I was in Greece for five weeks, and for security reasons they housed us together on a ship built in 1960. When I first arrived, I was taken to my room on the lowest level of this old cruise ship. It was right next to the diesel engine that was always running. I was given instructions to unpack and report back in an hour, I quickly unpacked and went to the watertight doors and started reading how to operate them.

"What are you doing?" another agent asked as he approached.

"Hey, we are at the lowest level of the ship and if something happens, the first thing that closes down are these big steel doors built in 1960," I said.

There was a series of levers and wheels you had to turn in order to open the door. "If something happens, I want to be sure I can get off the ship."

The rooms were incredibly small, but they did have a porthole— maybe five inches in diameter, just above the waterline. Because the room was so close to the engine room, it was incredibly noisy. Luckily, I met a woman on the equestrian team who gave me a pair of earplugs. The shower was so tight, once I turned on the water, the shower curtain would cling to me after a single touch, and eventually gripping my entire body; these were not deluxe accommodations!

I was fortunate to get a ticket to the opening ceremony, courtesy of the U.S. Olympic Committee. They had too many tickets. I was also fortunate enough to get a ticket to *Sport's Illustrated* beach party for all the Olympic athletes. It was absolutely beautiful. I learned later that someone on our detail tried to get into the party without a ticket, and he actually got into an altercation with a security guard. Thank God he was not arrested; that would've been an embarrassing international incident! The Greeks were uncomfortable giving away authority by letting us carry guns, and if this agent had been caught it would've been ugly.

At first, the Greek police were a little standoffish with us. I think it was because they felt insulted that they needed Americans to be their "babysitters." But once we got to know them, we developed a solid working relationship.

There were a lot of protesters in Greece, and many who just liked to destroy things. They were protesting about this and that, but when they were done, the results were smashed windows. Another interesting practice in Greece involved motor scooters. If you were on a scooter and hit by a car, no matter what you were doing on the scooter, the person who hit you was always wrong. When we were driving around Athens, we saw people lying in the street after being hit by a vehicle. It was crazy.

In our briefing at the U.S. Embassy, they said if you could only speak a little bit of the native language, the one thing you should know is, "Take me to a private hospital." Apparently, in Greece there are two types of hospitals—public and private. The people at the embassy told us if you want to survive, go to the private hospitals.

During the Games, I got to see some of the athletes in action while competing and when they were off duty. We also were invited to a U.S. Olympic Committee party at the Olympic House during the closing ceremony. It was a nice party and from the deck of the building you could see the Acropolis lit up at night. It was incredible.

It was an interesting trip and I met many fascinating people, including the president of the Olympic Committee of Iraq.

"How is your country doing?" I asked him, and what he told me, I found remarkable. "My people," he said, "are highly educated and want a democracy. Our country is rich, not only in oil but in water as well. I am very optimistic about the future."

He gave me a new perspective on the country. I remember riding on Athens' subway where people would come up and ask if I was an American. I would reply, "Yes, I am." I was confused after they would ask, "Why did you start this war?"

"We were attacked first," I would tell them.

"What do you mean you were attacked?" they'd reply with a look of wonder on their faces.

So, I'd tell them about 9/11. It was amazing to me how little information was reported about the impact on America and why we went to war.

I was happy the Games ended without incident. I was ready to come home, but really did have a good time.

Closing Out My Career

Delaware, believe it or not, was an interesting place to work. We came across all types of antique firearms—things such as bazookas, unexploded military ordinances, TNT sticks, Japanese machine guns and other weapons from World War II. I'm not certain why, maybe because many things were handed down from one generation to the next, I think I sent more firearms to the ATF firearms library while I was in Delaware than from any other place during my career.

Unfortunately, I didn't find the management in Delaware any better than the other stops of my career. Simply put, our management was vindictive. I recall one time a report maybe three fourths of an inch thick was sent back to me because it was missing two commas in the body of the report. The case was already adjudicated, or finished, and they marked where the two commas were to go. I put the commas in, then I put it through the computer's spell and grammar check; it told me to remove the two commas! It took about an hour to correct all three copies. What a waste of time, but that's ATF!

Across Delaware, some roads weren't marked as well as they should have been, although they did get better over the years. One day, when we couldn't find an address we went to a local fire department and they told us how to go. They told us there were no street signs, but when you see the chicken coops make a left! That was part of what made this job so great; you never knew where you were going to end up, what was going to happen next or how an investigation was going to unfold.

At this time, the state of Delaware was offering weapons of mass destruction courses, covering everything from radiation detection to downrange sampling for hazardous materials. We also did a lot of command and control training. Whatever course was offered, I would try to take it.

Following 9/11, the Federal Government was trying to train as many people as possible. They felt the more eyes they had the better off our country would be. We would also go to these training sessions to learn how terrorist cells worked, and to be updated on the latest trends.

I tried to incorporate any new intelligence into our race-day preparation. By now, the two NASCAR races in Delaware brought in more than 200,000 people and some $250 million to the community. As far as my casework during this time, the Bush administration ramped up the enforcement of federal firearms laws, and under this mandate, we were busy taking cases from the state to federal prosecution. It made our job much easier, because many of the criminals were being brought to us, as opposed to us having to do investigations and then arresting the violators.

In 2007, ATF finally settled with me on my EEO case, and I was allowed to join the NRT. That February, I began planning to do a memorial for the four agents killed when serving the warrant on the Branch Davidians. As ATF agency president for FLEOA, I met with the ATF director for our yearly meeting and asked if he would support a memorial on the 15th anniversary at Waco.

I was trying to think of what to do, because the state of Texas put a one-and-a-half ton bolder out on the street with a plaque on it remembering the four agents killed. Shortly after it was put on display it was stolen—rock and all—leaving no remembrance of any kind for those agents who died that day.

I was thinking of different ways to do this without the memorial being vandalized. Lucky for us, the city of Waco was also erecting a police memorial, one for all the men and women who died in the county—including the four ATF agents. I contacted the city, and learned the memorial was to be completed in January 2008. I asked them if we could have a memorial service there on February 28—the 15th anniversary. They agreed.

I offered to assist with fundraising, and they were more than happy to have the help. I obtained financial support from our association, which helped sponsor the event. Local governments and the state of Texas helped as well. They provided the honor guards, a bugler and rifle squads for the 21-gun salute.

When I first floated this idea with ATF they thought it was great, but I knew there would be trouble. I made sure all the permits and reservations were in my name, so I could control the activities. I had planned wisely. You wouldn't believe some of things I had to go through.

First, ATF wanted to move the event to D.C. I successfully convinced them that was a bad idea. They wanted to move the event away from the memorial site and have the service inside, forcing me to give up the room I reserved for the luncheon. It just went on and on.

Ultimately, ATF did agree to pay for chairs as well as other expenses that fell to the wayside. It was crazy, but I'm glad I did what I did. The ceremony went off without a hitch, and everyone enjoyed the barbecue held after the ceremony. It was great. I was honored that the monument committee allowed us to put a special remembrance dedicated to the fallen ATF agents on one of the benches. It's located in a place that's not readily visible unless you're at the memorial. The remembrance reads,"To our fallen brothers, you will never be forgotten. From your friends at ATF."

I consider pulling off that remembrance as my greatest accomplishment at ATF.

That December of 2008, I lost the first criminal court case of my career. There was a guy in Dover who had been arrested and qualified for a 924 E penalty—if caught with a gun after three previous felony convictions, you get 15 years in prison as a mandated sentence. For some reason, the U.S. attorney told me he wanted the original arresting officer to sit in the second chair. This officer had no experience in federal court. I was sequestered as a possible witness; I could not even sit in the courtroom during the proceedings. This really ticked me off, but the crazy thing was, even though we lost, the U.S. attorney's office selected me for an award for my work on this investigation.

It was about this time in my career that I began to think about retiring. In January 2009, President Obama's inauguration train trip stopped in Wilmington. I was assigned on the downrange HAZMAT team in case of an incident. This was great. It was the first time I had an assignment like this where I did not have to stand post in the freezing weather.

Now that I was on the NRT, I went to HAZMAT school to become a technician. It was another hard course that I didn't think I was going to survive, but did. The only call out I did as a member of the NRT team was when an individual burned down a church with a predominantly African-American congregation right after Obama was sworn in as president. I was the team photographer. It was interesting and a good experience working with the other team members.

On July 29, 2009, Delaware Senator Ted Kaufman honored me by reading my biography on the Senate floor. One of my greatest pleasures was to have my wife and mother by my side. The event is recorded for posterity in the official Congressional Record. It was in the 111th Congress, Volume 155, Number 116.

Several months before I retired, I went on my last arrest warrant. It was a big round up for the Latin street gang known as MS-13. I was assigned a new agent to work with that morning. He was a big guy with prior experience working as a deputy sheriff, I believe in Tennessee.

We had an arrest and search warrant for the subject's house. My partner and I were assigned to cover the rear of the house, while a local SRT served the initial warrant. When we arrived, we saw a car in front of the house with its engine running and loud music blaring from it. It was about 5:50 a.m., and at 6 o'clock we were going to serve the warrant.

All of a sudden, the brake lights came on and the subject was seen moving the car. We called it in and were told to sit tight. The house was on a corner lot, and the driveway was in the back of the house on another street. Fortunately, the suspect had pulled into the rear driveway and stopped right in front of his garage door. I was told over the radio that two agents would make the arrest and that the SRT was still going to clear the house before we would search it.

As my partner and I approached the car, I told the new agent to stand behind something as he was standing next to a tree and not behind it. The two agents then approached the vehicle, opened the door and tried to remove the subject. You could hear and see the struggle going on as they were wrestling with the target. This went on for about a minute, and the rear cover agents who were closest to the struggle did not move.

"Cover me," I hollered to my partner, as I went up to the vehicle to see if I could help. The two agents were still struggling to pull the suspect out of the car through the open door. He was so drunk, and just smiling and holding onto the steering wheel. I couldn't help them, because they were blocking the car's doorway. I went around to the other side of the door, reached into the car and struck the subject several times right below his wrists to see if I could get him to release the steering wheel. It didn't work.

I then began peeling his fingers off the steering wheel one at a time. When I finally got to the second hand, he let go and all three of them fell out of the car. The subject was fighting like a turtle on his back. He was swinging his arms and legs all over the place.

"Did you see anything on him?" I yelled at the two agents as we struggled with the guy. I was careful not to use the word "gun," because I didn't want anyone out there to get crazy.

In the tussle, I determined he had nothing on him. So I stepped on his midsection, reached across to his far side, grabbed his belt and shirt, lifted him up and flipped him over. My mistake was being too close to his body when I lifted him. I started falling back and had to let him go. The two other agents were just looking at him. I yelled, "Grab him!" as I stepped back.

My colleagues quickly put the handcuffs on him. While he was lying on his side, he was making a loud gagging sound. I asked who was transporting him to jail and an FBI agent said, "We are."

I warned them that he was going to throw up as soon as he was placed upright, and they should get him in a chair first and let him vomit before he got into the car. Then a DEA agent said, "Screw him."

"You're right," I said turning to him, but he was still going to throw up. There was a lawn chair less than two feet from where we were standing. I grabbed it, sat the drunken suspect in the chair, and he then threw up for about five minutes. The subject had a 1.5 liter bottle of vodka in his car, and by appearances, it seemed he drank the whole thing by himself except for maybe a quarter inch still swishing around the bottom of the bottle.

"What happened to you?" I asked my partner when it was all over.

"I was covering you," he said.

"Don't you ever let that happen again," I said. "There was no reason to let only three agents subdue a subject with all these other law enforcement officers around."

"But other agents were out there as well as me," he meekly retorted.

"But not ATF agents," I said with a look that concluded the discussion.

We entered the house to search it and began seizing all his assets. Some of the agents were headed home when the operation command center decided to remove these huge plasma screen TVs from the house. At the time there were only a few of us still there, and we were waiting for the FBI truck. The house had a long driveway, and the FBI agent driving the truck refused to make it easier for us to load the TVs by driving on the grass and getting the vehicle as close to the door as possible.

"You can either move these TVs by yourself, or move the f'ing truck," I yelled to him.

He moved the truck.

I think if I had any second thoughts about retiring, this incident settled it. Law enforcement had changed a lot since I started the job. Everyone now seemed to be afraid to lay hands on someone, even if a fellow officer needed help. It was crazy.

In December 2009, I retired. I could have worked longer, but honestly, I recognized I was beginning to have less patience, and I did not want to retire bitter like some of my colleagues.

It had been nearly 22 years since my first, snowy day with the agency. ATF management stayed consistent to the very end. On my first day, none of the photographs of my swearing in ceremony came out; I had no record of my official start with the agency. And now, on my retirement plaque, they misspelled my name and the retirement award wasn't ready for presentation at the party. I received it a couple weeks after I had officially retired.

I suppose the truth is it isn't about how it started or how it ended. I am very proud of my many accomplishments throughout my career. Right up to the very end, there was never a dull moment.

Epilogue

As a college student, if someone had suggested I would have a long career in law enforcement, I would have told him or her they were crazy. It's funny how life plays out. Today, I can't imagine having done anything else.

In preparing for this book, I spent countless hours over many years thinking back on the people with whom I worked and the many experiences ATF provided and the places the job took me. Even though I remain amazed at the consistent lack of decent management regardless of where I served, I had a good career and am proud to have worn the ATF badge.

I recognize that in certain situations—especially relating to Waco—my recollections differ from the published historical record. In most cases, I believe that's due to the fact that I was never fully debriefed as part of any investigation looking into ATF's Waco operations. I've tried to correct that through this book.

In addition, to help preserve the memory of my colleagues and friends who died at Waco, I've contributed a substantial portion of my law enforcement gear, documents and memorabilia to the National Law Enforcement Museum in Washington, D.C. I want future generations to have access to the most complete and accurate history of the Waco event as possible. I hope these items will help this new organization build a credible and interesting collection that commemorates the important work law enforcement officers perform every day across the country.

About the Authors

David DiBetta

Dave DiBetta's government career began in the early '80s after graduating with a Bachelor of Science degree from SUNY Fredonia. Dave enrolled in the U.S. Army and served in the military police where he represented First Army at the All-Army Pistol Championship. Following his military service, he worked for the IRS in the underwriter's program until he received a full-time position as a Customs Inspector at JFK International Airport in New York.  While at Customs, Dave applied for a position with Alcohol, Tobacco and Firearms, and for the next 22½ years he served as an ATF Special Agent.

During those years Dave received a number of commendations including the Director's Award, Distinguished Service Medal for valor, eight special act/service awards, and several letters of appreciation and on the spot awards. Over the years Dave was deployed to serve at numerous national and international events. Among the most significant assignments were Republican and Democrat National Conventions, the NATO 50th Anniversary celebration, a Middle East Peace Summit, a United Nations General Assembly meeting, two Olympic Games, a National Boy Scout Jamboree, and NASCAR Raceway security details. At the conclusion of his ATF career in 2009, Delaware U.S. Senator Kaufman read Dave's biography on the Senate floor.

Dave received extensive IED, WMD, Command and Control training during his career with ATF. He was a member of ATF's Special Response Team, and National Response Team, certified as a Hazmat Tech and was a Tactical Operations Officer. Dave also revitalized the local chapter for the Federal Law Enforcement Officers Association in Delaware. He became its chapter president before later serving as Agency President, representing all ATF agents nationwide.

Scott Fasnacht

As an award-winning corporate communications professional for more than 25 years, Scott Fasnacht has developed strategies and crafted copy that connects vision with opportunity for some of the world's most recognizable brands. He has led his own company, Aperture Communications, since 2006.

Noted for his deep business acumen and unique storytelling ability, Scott is highly regarded for transforming complex ideas and issues into messages that are easily understood and acted upon.

A native of Central Pennsylvania, he is a 1983 graduate of Franklin & Marshall College. In his spare time, Scott is a student of the American Civil War, an amateur photographer and fly-fisherman.

INDEX

D

DAD (Deputy Associate Director) 176
Dallas, Texas 89, 166, 167, 217
DCIP (Diverse Career Impact Program) 211, 212, 214
DEA (Drug Enforcement Administration) 117, 228
Defense Department 212
Delaware State Police 205, 207
Delaware State Trooper 208
Delgado, Bob 156
Detroit, Michigan 39, 40, 60
DiBetta, Judy 39
DiBetta, Pam 31, 33
DiBetta, Ron 33
Division Tactical Advisor 206
Dix, New Jersey 216

E

El Paso Fire Department 112
El Paso Intelligence Center 165
El Paso, Texas 165

F

Fasnacht, Scott 9, 234
FBI (Federal Bureau of Investigation) 23, 24, 25, 26, 27, 39, 115, 118, 120, 125, 126, 127, 148, 180, 182, 183, 188, 220, 222, 228, 229
Federal Law Enforcement Officers Association 234
FFL (Federal Firearms Licensee) 41, 82
FLEOA (Federal Law Enforcement Officers Association) 155, 156, 168, 221, 222, 225
FLETC (Federal Law Enforcement Training Center) 188
Fort Fisher 126
Fort Hood, Texas 89, 93, 94
Fort McClellan, Alabama 60, 188
Fort Meade 131
Fort Miles 130
Fort Sam Houston 128, 161

G

Gallo, Rich 156
Glynco, Georgia 31, 131, 188
Greece, Europe 222, 223, 224
Greek Police 223

H

Hansen, Kurt 156
Harris County Sheriff's Department 59
Hartnett, Daniel 115, 118
HAZMAT Team 227
Holbrook, New York 13
Honor Guard 162
Hostage Rescue Team 125
Houston, Texas 8, 31, 32, 33, 34, 35, 38, 39, 40, 41, 42, 44, 49, 57, 58, 60, 62, 67, 71, 72, 73, 76, 79, 87, 89, 108, 124, 128, 138, 167, 174, 177, 194

Rockville, Maryland 183
Rudolph, Eric 182

S

Salt Lake City, Utah 218
San Antonio, Texas 128, 161
Secret Service 69, 123, 193,
   194
SRT (Special Response Team)
   57, 59, 60, 64, 67, 73, 84, 88,
   89, 94, 111, 112, 118, 134,
   135, 136, 137, 138, 161, 170,
   173, 188, 199, 206, 216, 227,
   234
State Department 188, 200,
   207, 216, 217

T

TEA (Treasury Enforcement
   Agent) 211
Texas Department of Public
   Safety 116
Texas Protective Services 70
Texas Rangers 84, 109, 146
Texas State Trooper Honor
   Guard 148
Texas State Troopers 109, 162
Thibodeau, David 165
Thompson, Charlie 171
TOB (Tactical Operations
   Branch) 176, 185, 188, 201
TOO (Tactical Operations
   Officer) 63, 64, 67, 68, 71,
   89, 91, 103, 109, 125, 166,
   170, 173, 180, 185, 187, 199,
   221, 234
TSA (Transportation Security
   Agency) 218, 219

TSTC (Texas State Technical
   College) 73, 74
Tulsa, Oklahoma 218
Tyler, Texas 173

U

U.S. Armed Forces 87
U.S. Army 7, 180, 233
U.S. Attorney's Office 35, 36,
   50, 227
U.S. Customs 7, 19, 29, 42, 43,
   44, 67, 72, 124, 131, 180,
   193, 194
U.S. Government 222
U.S. Law Enforcement 107
U.S. Marshals 128, 207
U.S. Military 169

W

Waco, Texas 8, 69, 71, 72, 73,
   83, 84, 87, 89, 94, 111, 112,
   115, 120, 121, 123, 125, 126,
   128, 139, 142, 144, 149, 150,
   156, 164, 165, 170, 171, 176,
   177, 178, 195, 225, 226, 231
Washington, D.C. 8, 73, 84,
   87, 115, 124, 171, 172, 174,
   175, 177, 178, 183, 185, 193,
   194, 215, 217, 218, 220, 226,
   231
Williams, Robert J. 157, 160
Willis, Steven David 77, 80,
   96, 103, 109, 110, 118, 120,
   121, 122, 157, 160